My Life in Red and White

Arsène Wenger was born in Strasbourg in 1949 and was an acclaimed manager of football clubs in France and Japan before unexpectedly being appointed manager of Arsenal in 1996, where he enjoyed unmatched success. He resigned in 2018 and is now Chief of Global Development for FIFA. He lives in north London and Paris.

My Life in Red and White

MY AUTOBIOGRAPHY

Arsène Wenger

Translated by
Daniel Hahn and Andrea Reece

First published in France as *Ma Vie en Rouge et Blanc* by
Editions Jean-Claude Lattès 2020

First published in Great Britain in 2020
by Weidenfeld & Nicolson
This paperback edition published in 2021 by Weidenfeld & Nicolson
An imprint of The Orion Publishing Group Ltd
Carmelite House, 50 Victoria Embankment
London EC4Y 0DZ

An Hachette UK Company

1 3 5 7 9 10 8 6 4 2

A CIP catalogue record for this book
is available from the British Library.

ISBN (Mass Market Paperback) 978 1 4746 1826 7
ISBN (eBook) 978 1 4746 1827 4

Typeset by Input Data Services Ltd, Somerset

Printed in Great Britain by Clays Ltd, Elcograf S.p.A.

www.orionbooks.co.uk
www.weidenfeldandnicolson.co.uk

CONTENTS

'all things excellent are as difficult as they are rare'

Ethics, Spinoza

'to try to make men aware of the greatness they do not know they have in themselves'

The Temptation of the West, André Malraux

PROLOGUE

I left Arsenal on 13 May 2018.

The club had been my whole life for twenty-two years. It was my passion, my constant preoccupation. Thanks to Arsenal, I was able to pursue my managerial career in exactly the way I wanted: I was able to influence players' lives, to instil a playing style in the club, and to experience some truly wonderful victories. I had a freedom and a power that managers no longer have today.

Leaving the club after all those incredible, intense, unforgettable years, and losing the intensity of that power, was difficult. Arsenal is still a part of me: I say 'my club' when I'm talking about it and, even though it's in other hands now, I am still as passionate as ever about the club, about the supporters, about the players who are selected, coached, supported, and pushed to give their best. What matters to me are the game and the men, those moments of grace that football offers to those who love it and who give it their all.

Matches won are precious memories, and matches lost, the ones I still don't dare watch again, continue to haunt me even many years later: what should we have done? What happened? My whole life has swung between loving victory and despising defeat.

I am passionate about football and that passion has never dimmed.

When I arrived at Arsenal, the English didn't know who I was. The question *Arsène who?* came up time and again. I understood. I was only the fourth foreign manager in the history of top-flight English football. The first three had had mixed fortunes. The English codified the rules of football just as the French perfected wine. We don't often ask an English person to come over to make Bordeaux. For twenty-two years, I tried to make the truth of the game and the pitch prevail. I had already known defeat, disappointments, huge anger, departures, and fantastic players, but no team had become part of me quite like this one.

The club changed so much, and I changed with it, and football has changed with us. My kind of football, the conditions in which I pursued my passion, the freedom I had, my longevity as the manager of a club, these things have all but disappeared. I am not sure a player today who still didn't have a club at fourteen, or a coach until he was nineteen, could go from the French departmental championships to Ligue 1 and play so many matches and have so many adventures. And nor am I sure that a manager nowadays could have overall management responsibility for a team like Arsenal and choose his players in the way I did, with total freedom and total involvement. I was fortunate, but I know what sacrifices I made, too.

In recent years, football has undergone many profound transformations. Some of the changes, I think, are more striking than others: the increasing number of foreign owners; the emergence of social media with its demands and excesses; the unremitting pressure on and isolation of players and managers, at a time when expectations have never been higher. Football has changed a great deal both pre- and post-match, notably with more analysis of the game. But one thing does not change: the 90 minutes still belong to the player, 90 minutes during which he is king.

European football is no longer dominated by three clubs, as it once was. The other teams have moved up to their level.

Analysts have taken on a very prominent role and are involved in matches right from half-time, making it possible to understand the game better, and to have objective criteria for analysing the match, whereas previously everything had been left to the subjectivity of the manager. Nevertheless, the manager remains the sole decision maker.

Statistics and science must be a part of performance analysis, but they need to be used in combination with a deep knowledge of the game. The latest studies show that players are demoralised by too great a use of statistics, no doubt because they feel their individuality is lost in the process.

More than ever, a manager is responsible for a team's results even though he does not always have the means to influence every decision. Comments about him are always exaggerated one way or the other: 'He's brilliant', or 'He's rubbish'.

We are often involved in these transformations without really being aware that they are happening, and we remain focused on what we believe. But today I have emerged from my bubble and everything seems clearer to me: the unjustified attacks, the exaggerations, the loneliness of the manager. I read *L'Équipe* every day, I watch two, sometimes three matches a day, I listen and wonder how what's being said can be fair, why certain things happen as they do, where the truth of the game lies, and I do the same with my life, my commitments, my passion.

I look at all these changes and I think about them, and yet I always see football for what it is and what it should be: a match where anything can happen, the players, 90 minutes, fantastic moves, an element of luck, talent, courage, a touch of magic and, for those who are watching these men play, the search for excitement, for a memory, for a lesson in life.

Football exists under the pressure to perform. You need to know how to take a step back, to analyse things from above. A club depends on three things in order to grow: strategy, planning and application.

I have been playing since I was a child. I've known amateur clubs with players and coaches who played wonderful football, who were excited about every match, who talked about nothing but football, who were capable of crossing France on a second-class sleeper train to play a match then travelling back to Strasbourg in the early hours of the morning to go straight in to work at a factory, without complaining, without any expectations other than playing and winning the next match. That creates lifelong bonds, and the coaches from those teams have been my mentors. They were passionate, and realistic, too, and they knew how to communicate their love of the game.

Playing is still a source of joy for me today. Like all those who play football at any level, I continue to rediscover the excitement I felt as a child.

A day without a football match seems empty to me. I still enjoy watching football because I want to carry on learning, thinking, trying to progress in my understanding of the game and what can be offered to a player to help him evolve. But in the past few months, I have occasionally skipped watching a match with one of my favourite teams on television, or some other match I hope will be interesting. Instead of this sacrosanct time dedicated to football, I spend an evening with my daughter or my friends. Previously, that would have been impossible. So now I have some more peaceful moments when I notice the beauty around me, be it the countryside, a city like London, or like Paris where I am spending more and more time.

For thirty-five years, I lived like a top athlete, obsessed by my passion. I didn't go to the theatre or the cinema; I neglected those around me. For thirty-five years, I didn't miss a single match, a single cup, a single championship, which meant living with an iron discipline, and I continue to live like that today: I get up at 5:30 a.m., do my exercises, train, eat and drink the way my former players did. I no longer know if this is a choice or a habit that imprisons me. But it's the only way for me to live. Without it, I think I would be unhappy. If happiness is liking the life one lives, I can say I have been happy, and still am.

For all those years, the only thing that counted for me was the next match and the result. For all those years, all I wanted was to win. My time and my thoughts were taken up with this sole objective. I was only really there when I was on the pitch. With other people, with those that I love, I was often elsewhere. I either saw nothing or I saw everything in red and white, the colours of all the teams

6

that I have coached: Nancy, Monaco, Nagoya, Arsenal. I did not see beauty or pleasure or relaxation. The idea of taking holidays, having a good time, never occurred to me, or hardly ever. Even my nights were filled with dreams of football. I dreamt about upcoming matches, about the advice I could give, about the two or three players I was never sure of: should I play them immediately, or let them go; calm their frustrations, carry on motivating them? They were my ghosts.

I say to my friends jokingly that grass – the grass on the pitch of the stadium onto which I walked out so often, which can change the outcome of a match, which I took obsessive care of, which I talked about every morning with the club groundsman – is my only drug. It makes them laugh, but it's totally true. It is my drug. Since I left Arsenal, I have turned down clubs where I thought I would not have the same freedom, the same power. FIFA made me an offer that I accepted because it is a new challenge and an effective way of reflecting on my sport and working with a team. Until such time, maybe, that I find myself back in the heaven and hell of a manager's job.

I want to share what I know, what I have learnt about the game and the sport, and pass it on to those who love it, to those who know it but also to those who are less familiar with the power and beauty of football and who wonder how we succeed, how we lead men to victory, what we learn from defeats for ourselves and for others. I would like to contribute to creating a structure for our game around the world. And to ensure that wherever it comes from, talent can be spotted and developed.

Today, my former players are not my only ghosts, and upcoming matches are no longer my only dreams.

After the death of my sister, my brother Guy died a few months ago. He was my big brother. He was five years older than me. He played football before I did, and it was with him that I first played: in our bedroom above our parents' bistro, in the streets of our village and in the Duttlenheim football club. They are dreams of when we were starting out, the moments on which everything hinged, when I was the youngest but very determined. I would fight to play with my brother and his friends.

They are dreams of childhood, in an Alsace that still feels like home to me, an Alsace that shaped my personality.

They are dreams in which the only language I hear spoken is the Alsatian German dialect.

They are dreams that take me back to where it all began.

'It's practically my first memory: I'm watching our team play, I'm keeping my distance, I'm watching with faith and passion, I'm holding a prayer book and praying for victory . . . Years later, I replaced the prayer book with good players.'

1

THE CHILD WHO DREAMT
ABOUT FOOTBALL

I've always suffered from the intensity of my desires, even if I didn't know where the feelings came from. They undoubtedly originated in the Alsace village where I grew up: Duttlenheim, a few kilometres from Strasbourg. It's a village that no longer exists: the years have passed and everything has changed. I am the child of another century and another era: the streets I used to know, and where I first played football, the men who educated me, among whom I grew up, the football pitch that hosted our club's matches, the spirit that reigned there, the way children used to grow up – it's all changed so much. It was a village of farmers, where the horse ruled supreme. There were three blacksmiths. Today there are none.

I come from that world, from that village that was like an island, and the man I would become, the player I was, the manager, this man who thinks only of football, was moulded, shaped by the spirit of those places and by the men who lived there. I lived in a world dominated by the cult of physical effort.

In those days, the village was shut off from the rest of the world, like all villages in Alsace, and dominated by religion. Down the generations the names tended to stay the same, and we were known by my mother's family name – 'the Metzes'. Life fitted into the pocket handkerchief-sized space between the bistro, the school, the church, the town hall, the shops and the football ground that was two kilometres from the train station where nobody ever went: why would anyone leave that haven, that world where everyone helped everyone else? All around the village were fields where I spent a lot of time at the weekends and during the school holidays. That was where I learnt to do hard physical work, to milk the cows, just like my grandparents and my parents' friends did. It was a world of small farmers where physical strength was respected and admired. The men I knew worked the earth, lived off it, and I really loved those people. They earned no more than a meagre living, certainly. It was subsistence farming where the crops were mostly tobacco, wheat, rye, beetroot and potatoes. It was tractor-less agriculture – tractors didn't arrive in the village until 1963, when I was fourteen – relying solely on the strength of men and horses. My paternal grandparents had one horse. Having two was already a sign of affluence.

These were tough, taciturn men, who would go to mass on Sunday mornings and to my parents' modest bistro whenever they could. The village was all they knew of the world. It was here that their friendships were formed, and their romances, it was here that they worked, here their children grew up.

In this closed world, we children were free, we were never afraid, we trusted one another. Whenever we did anything stupid or wrong, it was reported by word of mouth and immediately punished. Religion gave us a very clear sense of what was right, of morality, of truth. We village children were always together, growing up on the streets and in the fields, but the dreams we had were not the same.

My father was one of the men from that village: he was a rational man, deeply attached to his village, an incredibly hard-working and religious man. Profoundly good and understanding. He gave me a road-map for life, with values that gave me incredible strength to face any trials and the worst betrayals. He had been a part of those numerous '*malgré-nous*', the people from the area who'd been forcibly conscripted ('*against our will*') to fight with the Germans against their own country. He never spoke about the war, but I always admired his bravery, his modesty, and I knew what terrible trials he must have been through. I was born after the war, on 22 October 1949, and like all the children in the region my childhood was permeated with that post-war atmosphere, the tragedy every family had lived through.

My father had worked at Bugatti between the ages of fourteen and seventeen, then in the bistro with my mother, before setting up his own auto parts business in nearby Strasbourg. He never took a day off, never had a week's holiday. His day began at 7 a.m. in the bistro, then he'd work at his company, and when he got back at 8 p.m., he would go on working at the bistro. This was where the football club met, and where the club's results and forthcoming matches were posted. Every Wednesday evening, the committee of the football club, which had been established in 1923, would put together the team for the following Sunday's match. Watching the way we played non-stop, and seeing how passionate we were about it, and that we weren't too bad, my father had formed the youth team where my brother and I started out.

My father definitely liked football, even if he never said as much. To him it was a pastime for livening up the village, a few fine battles, a distraction, but it wasn't a constant dream for him as it was for the other men of the village, it wasn't an all-consuming passion. He and my mother never dreamt that my brother or I would become players: it was inconceivable. My brother was talented, he played as a midfielder and a central defender. Everything was there and yet he was lacking something, a key, something that didn't quite click: faith. Football, to all of them, was a pastime. Full stop. Not a job. A job is more serious, something that allows you to earn a living, and that wasn't the case with football.

During those years, I remember a prevailing atmosphere of hard work and enjoyment, and we did both of those things to the full.

As a child, I was absolutely free, and often very alone. My mother would recall: 'We used to leave you in your room and not worry about you.' Perhaps that's where my independence comes from. In any time left between school, the fields and the church, I played football whenever I could, on the streets and in the yards and the gardens that taught me so much. I played like the other children, like my older brother, like the men of my village must have played, the way my maternal uncles used to talk about it, but football was already occupying all my thoughts and turning slowly but surely into an obsession.

It's practically my first memory: I'm watching our team play, I'm keeping my distance, I'm watching with faith and passion, I'm holding a prayer book and praying for victory, I'm five or six years old. Is it possible that I knew, despite my young age, that we weren't any good and that it would take a miracle, some help from God, the support of my faith, to make us win? Is it possible that I knew, despite my young age and those impossible dreams, that football would become my only religion, my only hope: a match won, a victory, a beautiful and respected game? Did I already have, perhaps, that fierce desire to win? Years later, I replaced the prayer book with good players and being well prepared for the likelihood of winning – reason instead of faith.

I have another memory that is a good illustration of this hoping for victory. I would often spend hours in the fields with a farmer who let me work alongside him or who would take a rest while I gave him a hand. His name was Adolphe Kocher. We talked football, we discussed the team's disappointing results, we went back over the match. One day, he claimed that he was a brilliant player himself and that with him on board the team was going to dazzle, that we'd be victorious at last. 'You'll see, kid, I'll play in the next match.' I spent the following few days waiting for the next match, imagining how he would play, dreaming of the goals he'd score. But he had lied to me: he didn't play in the next match. Everything fell apart. I was that little boy who wanted to win at all costs, who could think of nothing but coming first, nothing but victory.

My parents' bistro was the beating heart of that village. It was like so many Alsatian bistros: open every day, heated by a stove in the middle, about twenty tables, filled with men who drank one beer after another and smoked unfiltered Gauloises and talked non-stop about football: their team, the neighbouring team, the team they would be up against next, and the team they so admired, Racing Club de Strasbourg, which fired them up, made them smoke more and drink more and then so often shout, and fight, and fall.

That bistro, La Croix d'Or, was my school: I listened to their conversations, I noticed which man talked loudest, which one lied, who was the conceited one and who the retiring one, their forecasts, their rages, their analyses. It was actions that counted, not words. Was this already a school for observing individuals and how groups worked? Definitely. I just remember those men who talked so much while my father was so silent. As a child, when I used to walk across the bistro, and later at around ten, twelve years old, when I would sometimes serve there, I would be constantly listening, watching, attempting to understand. If I came to love players, managers, all real enthusiasts, if I loved listening to them and working out what sort of men they were, I owe that to the customers at the bistro, to the men of my village. I retained their fervour, but not their excesses: alcohol, brawling, violence, everything that used to scare or disgust me as a child. It was hard to see people I admired, my father's customers, drinking so much and sometimes turning violent. They needed to be restrained. That made a huge impression on me. But it gave me strength and an incredible instinct.

When I left that smoke-filled room, I would make my

way into the apartment upstairs where we lived. We were a family without my having any understanding of what that word meant: my parents worked from morning to night, both of them at the bistro, or my mother in the bistro and my father at his car parts business. They had started working at fourteen. My mother had been orphaned very young. They were models of courage and tenacity, resilient people who did not complain. We never ate together and we talked very little. My sister was ten years older than me and my brother five: I was the little one, the one everybody wanted to protect but also the one left to fend for himself, the child who watches and imitates and tries to grow up faster.

On each floor of our house, I had a perfect observation post: invisible, hidden, noting the failings and excesses of my elders, taking the best from them, their experiences, their passions, their relentless effort, understanding the bravery of their lives, lives that were simple and modest and uncomplicated, men with dreams that were limited by their horizons and who could not leave. I was curious, and doubtless more impatient than the others to discover other towns, other regions. I'd figured out that I was living in the midst of men who were soon going to lose their way of life, their habits, their simple faith. I felt that I wanted to escape, even if it meant bearing the weight of guilt for that leaving. I wasn't abandoning them. It remained my world, though my parents, brother and sister undoubtedly suffered from my moving away, from that passion that swept everything away with it. They never said as much. They didn't often praise, nor did they reproach or articulate their suffering. I imagine it hit my brother the hardest. But we remained very close and, when I was at Arsenal, he watched every match and screamed at me like a big brother does whenever he thought I had got something wrong.

In the village, we didn't have much. I sometimes wonder whether my passion might not have been born out of that frustration: that small world, those so scarce words we exchanged, those matches our team lost, that pitch that had so little in common with real football pitches did, like the one in Strasbourg where one of my uncles used to take me twice a year, those tears I shed with each defeat.

I've met a lot of players in my career who did not come through the traditional youth academies or experienced early rejection before later finding success, men for whom football became an impossible dream but who found their way back in with their heads held high, like Olivier Giroud, Laurent Koscielny, N'Golo Kanté, Franck Ribéry – the list goes on.

When I think about my childhood, I have very specific memories.

We played on the streets.

We played with no jerseys, no coach, and no referee. Having no jerseys was invaluable because it forced us to look up and develop our peripheral vision, to acquire vision that was deeper. Having no coach, when young, was also invaluable for allowing us to develop a game based on taking the initiative. Have we perhaps drifted to the opposite extreme today?

We would put together a team at random or according to the wishes of the two captains of the moment, who were often the two best players.

I played with children my own age who have remained cherished friends, like Joseph Metz, the Burels, the Geistels and Hugues Chales. We were very like one another, we had the same schooling, the same codes. But I also played with older players, who were the same age as my big brother or older still. And when you play with older children, you have to be resilient, cunning, not afraid. With the children my age and the older ones, I quickly understood that I could get by and be accepted.

We knew instinctively who was good, who had played well, whom we could count on.

We played to enjoy ourselves and that counted as much as victory.

Matches often ended in abuse or brawling. When we were injured there was no sub, you finished the match a passenger on the wing. You needed to survive, grit your teeth.

My brother and I would train in our bedroom, on the street in front of our house, in the garden behind the bistro, constantly. Yet we didn't talk. He saw me as a little kid. The only certain way of being with him was to play and to play well.

We would set off on foot towards what passed for a stadium, and when we were playing a team from another village, we would walk over to their ground, like a journey from one world to another.

It was the football of low-level amateurs, glorious, free, joyful, passionate. The matches were sometimes interrupted by one of us deserting because we had to do our homework, or have lunch, or learn the catechism, which used to infuriate me. It was an education in resourcefulness, in tenacity, in passion, in physical effort. I owe it a lot.

So when there was an end-of-season tournament organised in the village between four teams, the priest would bless the teams and the players would change in my parents' bistro before going to parade past. It was our World Cup. There were other great joys that came later, but that one has left its mark on me for ever.

I think about a story told by a Serbian player I very much admired. He must have lived in a village that was like mine but even poorer, far from everything, lost in the Yugoslavian countryside. When he was small, his uncle had given him a fabulous, shiny-white new ball. In order not to spoil it, he and his brother decided never to let it bounce on the ground and play only with their heads. There was only one ball, and they had to make it last. During one match, he was spotted by a coach from Red Star Belgrade. He was recruited thanks to the skills he had developed playing with his head in this way. What sort of player would he have been if he'd had access to twenty balls?

Not spoiling the ball he was given, playing all the time, developing his own qualities through perseverance and training: I liked everything about this story. The white ball was sacred to me, too, and it remains so to this day.

That was the kind of football I came from. If I'd had parents who were football enthusiasts and who'd encouraged me, if from the age of five I'd been at a school with a coach and had been given instructions, if I'd read all the manuals, watched every possible match on TV, what kind of player, what kind of manager would I have been? Football wasn't something I watched on television because we didn't have one. Except sometimes at school, where each child brought in one franc and we would watch a match on the black and white TV. It's possible that school was where I saw the final of the European Cup in 1960, aged ten: Real Madrid won 7-3 against Eintracht Frankfurt, their fifth European Cup in a row. In those days, Racing Club de Strasbourg was the team I supported, along with the German club Borussia Mönchengladbach. But I just loved Real Madrid. I thought it the strongest, the most beautiful, the most impressive of all clubs. The players were all in white, looking magnificent. There were players I admired, like Kopa, Puskás and Di Stéfano. It really was the dream club. Years later, when

I was managing Arsenal, I was twice offered the chance to take over at Real. It's terrible to have to turn down your childhood club. But I had a mission at Arsenal, a contract to honour, and I'd given my word. Besides, I must be the manager who has said no the most times: to PSG, to Juventus, to the national teams of both France and Japan. And each time was hard, but a commitment is a commitment. I'm sure that moral code is another thing I got from my childhood.

Football was a distant, inaccessible world, and nobody around me ever believed it might become my world, my life. Deep down, I hoped football would always occupy the number one spot in my heart, because without that dream, I was sure I would be miserable: unlike the others in my village, I wanted to leave, to step out onto a real pitch, to experience real battles.

They were years of hopes and discoveries.

When I talk to players who have come from a long way away, the ones from Africa especially, I know and recognise the vital importance of their childhoods, of the places they grew up, the ways those places shaped their bodies and their personalities. Alsace, and that childhood, gave me behavioural and moral codes, and stamina. But they shaped me physically, too. Some traces still remain: I have for example got a hollow at the top of my spine, a hollow that led some doctors to say I would be in a wheelchair at forty. Apparently it might have been due to having carried very heavy sacks of coal. The hollow is still there, it didn't interfere with my running as a player, and I'm still standing.

Of course to be a good football player, technique does matter, and that's something you acquire young, when you're between seven and twelve, but it's not enough on its own: not being afraid, knowing how to take the initiative, being resilient, reliable, showing solidarity, being a bit crazy, having one hell of a passion – I'm sure you acquire those things when young, too.

I know that as a child I was already hungry to know myself, to confront my limits, to surpass them. And football was my tool for doing this. I didn't want to suffer from my physical and mental inadequacies, I wanted rather to understand them, and overcome them. Coming from my village, speaking only Alsatian, I didn't understand much at school and I didn't work at all. My parents were very busy, so I was used to running wild and my behaviour at school was very much that of a 'tourist'. Fortunately I had a sudden wake-up call at fifteen, and caught up on the whole curriculum on my own. I discovered that if I worked hard I could achieve something. I passed my baccalaureate, then an economics degree at the University of Strasbourg. The subjects I chose to study allowed me to get a better understanding of how clubs worked, how they draw up their budgets, plan their investments, and purchase players. And later still, I took a three-week language course in Cambridge, at the age of 29, to learn to be confident in English. I was sure that would come in useful to me in football.

When I was fourteen, the age of Catholic confirmation, that momentous age at which according to the men in the village you become a man, you head off to work in the factory or the fields, and you are given a cigarette and a watch, everything changed. I didn't start working in the factory but I did receive a watch. I took to smoking much later in Cannes with my friend Jean-Marc Guillou when we used to spend hours talking football every night.

My parents sold the bistro. My mother stopped working and my father worked full-time in his business. We moved into a village house that my father had built. What has stayed with me, right up until today, was the football with the Duttlenheim youth team, the bistro, the football clubs, and the lessons I'd learnt.

'In the 1960s, my brother and I were playing in the Duttlenheim football team . . . We played in red and white. Fate would have it that those would be the colours of every team I would later coach.'

2

THE YOUNG MAN WHO
PLAYED FOOTBALL

In the 1960s, my brother and I were playing in the Duttlenheim football team. We were good, but I felt that everything was still to be done, to be proved. The club told us we were talented, indeed among the best in the village, but that didn't count for much. Our club played at the lowest rung of departmental football, and we often lost. But I do remember that when we organised ourselves – we had no coach – and put as much passion into it as possible, there were some fine victories and some wonderful mutual support, some yelling between players and an education in resourcefulness, in initiative.

We played in red and white. Fate would have it that those

would be the colours of every team I would later coach.

We didn't train; we just played, in a rather chaotic fashion, on Wednesday evening to prepare for the Sunday match. There was a committee that drew up the team list for the next match and that was it. The village was only just starting to have electrical lighting that made it possible to train in the evenings. Years later, when I got to know other clubs, other divisions, teams that were better prepared and better coached, I discovered the strengths and weaknesses that those years in Duttlenheim had left me with. I paid for that particularly with a lack of physical training. All us lads came from the same village – with the exception of one or two others from outside who played with us because the club and the village were gradually opening up – and between us, we had never done a single training session, we'd never done running exercises.

I think I made up for this lack of preparation, of seriousness in the team and of coaching through hard work, with an inordinate passion. I played to win and not just to entertain myself or because it was the only distraction in the village, along with the local dance where I was also very good. I remember that nobody taught me to dance: you learnt by asking a girl, by throwing yourself into it, by forgetting to be afraid. Like swimming. There was no swimming teacher like there is today, either: somebody would throw you in the water and you just had to figure it out for yourself.

At each Sunday match I felt I was playing for my life.

I was tense before and after every match and I was sometimes a very sore loser, but during the match I felt free: I was
exceptionally energetic and I gradually discovered that
I liked that extreme tension I felt before each encounter,
just as I liked those 90 minutes on the pitch. I was totally
absorbed by the game, in the bubble of the game, and nothing could distract me. Sometimes, for example, I wouldn't
notice it was raining till the match was over, when I returned
to the dressing room totally drenched. I liked the effort, I
liked pitting myself against it, against the pain: feeling pain,
struggling, running faster, the whole time, that was a part of
the game, of the art. Even in Duttlenheim I was constantly
pushing myself to do better. This served me very well when
I had to prove myself elsewhere and correct my technical
failings – like receiving the ball, for example, when my
first touch was not as precise as I would have wanted, and
my physical strength was likewise inadequate. But what
mattered most lay elsewhere, and that was something I
understood from my first steps in our humble team. I liked
playing, expressing myself on the pitch, surpassing myself,
working flat out. I liked the duels, going one-on-one. I was
tenacious, and I had stamina. I quickly understood that my
tactical analysis of the game was good, too.

During those years, with those players, some of whom are
still friends of mine, we experienced some victories that
were the pride of the village!

Yet it was not a victory that would change my life, but a defeat. A total thrashing: 7-1.

I was playing midfield with the Duttlenheim team against the AS Mutzig team, coached by Max Hild. AS Mutzig was in a different world from FC Duttlenheim. A coach, a team that played in the CFA, the French amateur league, a serious team that prepared in the way we did not. We were in the third departmental division, they in the third national division.

The match was a disaster for us and I was furious with myself, and disappointed. I knew some of the players in the opposing team, notably Jean-Marie Duton, likewise a midfielder, who has remained a friend and who told me this story. Max Hild went into the dressing room, congratulated them for winning the match, and then added: 'But most importantly today I've seen a great player, a first-rate midfielder.' Jean-Marie Duton stood up, thinking he was the man Max was praising. But he was talking about me, the midfielder of the defeated opposing team. Jean-Marie has always held that against me a bit, and yet that's never prevented us from having a very fine friendship. He took consolation in repeating, not without humour, that he got his revenge by marrying my first girlfriend.

That, too, was what football was about in those days: rivalry between teams, and mutual respect, and friends for life.

*

After that match, everything changed. I joined AS Mutzig in 1969: I finally discovered coaching, a new dimension, new stakes, new challenges. And most of all, a coach who became like a football father to me, and my role model.

Max Hild was born in 1932. He had grown up in Alsace and been shaped by it. And he was a great lover of football. He had started playing at Weyersheim, where he was born. And then he had experienced the fine team of Racing Club de Strasbourg and Ligue 1, the top tier in French professional football. He had also played at Bischwiller, at Wittisheim, and at Mutzig where he became a coach. He had learnt on the job. He was already a good player in the number 6 shirt, a *distributeur* midfielder linking defence and attack. But it was in 1966, while he was coaching at Mutzig, the club sponsored by the Wagner brewery, that he became a tactician with a love of the game, a unique vision and an ability to spot talented players, and help them develop.

He was a short man, five foot six, with a very strong Alsatian accent, good-natured, kind-hearted, with a curiosity and a passion for football that ignited and developed the passion that I had inside me. He sensed my impatience, my eagerness to progress, to play, to learn. And he gave me that unique opportunity to play. He didn't talk much. He never told me, for example, why he had spotted me and singled me out in that match: his answer, his praise and his encouragement were all related to the game.

It is thanks to Max and to what I had within me that I became a good player, and it's also thanks to him, I think, that I became a coach. After Mutzig, I played at Mulhouse, Vauban, and most significantly at Strasbourg, for Racing. I met wonderful coaches like Paul Frantz who coached Mulhouse, and Gilbert Gress who had been at Strasbourg with Max and who'd played in their French cup-winning side. They were all crazy about the game, they were the epitome of Alsatian football and they had a rigour, a sense of pushing one's limits, a burning desire to play. They all knew and really rated one another. Paul Frantz had coached Gilbert Gress as a player at Strasbourg, Max Hild had played against Gilbert Gress at amateur level, Gilbert Gress had brought Max Hild over to be a coach at Strasbourg's *centre de formation* or training academy, and Max brought me with him. I love those connections, those crossing paths, that mutual support. It was an era when loyalty and friendship mattered. And so I followed Max everywhere after Mutzig. Whenever he called, I would follow. It is really he who most shaped and influenced me. He died in 2014. Some of us players from that era visited his grave where each of us, in silence, told him what we owed him.

At Mutzig, Max had managed to bring men together and create a unique atmosphere. That connection, those friendships between players and with him, endured. We played, we trained, we ate our meals together, we talked football.

We were almost always together, and I learnt a lot. And yet, at first, nothing was easy.

I needed to adapt to the change of pace. Suddenly we were training twice a week, and as I had never done this before, I really threw myself into the training and by Saturday I was shattered.

I was filled with doubt. I wasn't sure I was up to it. In training, the other players tested me. They tripped me to see how I would react: would I go down, would I protest, would I bottle out? That was where I learnt that in the dressing room you should be able to quickly tell your teammates: 'You can count on me.' I learnt to make my presence felt. To fight.

I also learnt to transform my doubts into strength. I didn't want fear – the fear of being judged by others and the fear of consequences – to paralyse me on the pitch, to prevent me from moving forwards.

Max's role was important here, too. At Mutzig, at first, I was nothing special, I struggled to carve out a place for myself, but to his credit, Max persisted. He kept me in the team. He played me. It was a lesson: you must give players time. It's one of the shortcomings today: the players are better prepared but they have less time.

At each new club, I needed to relearn, to prove myself once again, to overcome my inadequacies. But I was hot-tempered. And I quickly understood, at Mutzig, at

Mulhouse, at Vauban, at Strasbourg, at all the clubs where I played and then at all the clubs where I coached, that life is a journey punctuated with afflictions that help us progress with our fears, our inner moods and emotions.

After Mutzig, I was signed by FC Mulhouse in 1973. That was where I met Paul Frantz. And just like in Mutzig, it was difficult to begin with. The first year was the hardest. I struggled to find my bearings, I got injured. I could no longer find the confidence, the success, the support that I had had at Mutzig. But the second year I was fully present. Meanwhile, I'd carried on training, persevering, making progress. It had paid off, and most importantly it had given me a place in the team that I hadn't expected. When the club went through financial difficulties, the players designated me, along with two others, to negotiate salaries and bonuses with the club president. That might have been the first time I negotiated and talked about money while thinking both about the interests of the club and the players. We reached an agreement. We would draw 50 per cent of our salary during the season, and if we managed to avoid relegation, we would get the rest. I thought we had found a fair and balanced compromise that was acceptable to everybody. But I later learnt that some players had broken ranks and gone to see the president to negotiate their individual cases, and had continued to draw their full salaries. And because I left at the end of the season to follow Max

Hild to ASPV Strasbourg, commonly known as Vauban, the remaining 50 per cent of my salary that was due to be paid to me never was.

Mulhouse, then, was an excellent school to prepare me for the next instalment in my career: I liked negotiating, thinking about the group, being a bridge between the players and the directors; I liked the sacrifices, the feeling that we really deserved our salaries. And there would be times when I would encounter lies, betrayals and some low blows.

After three seasons at Vauban, thanks once again to Max Hild, I became a player at Ligue 1 club RC Strasbourg in 1978. My dream was coming true. This was the club that had so fascinated us as children, the club we had thought so far out of reach. As a result, I wanted to give it everything I had. I was the first in to training, and I would have trained four times a day if I'd had to. I spent my life at the stadium, and I was living on Rue de Rome, just ten minutes from the club. I didn't count the hours I was working but it didn't feel like I was making a sacrifice. It seemed obvious: that was where I wanted to be.

At Strasbourg I was simultaneously a player, the man in charge of the training academy and the head of the youth team. It was thanks to Max Hild that I started to divide my time between being a player and being a young coach. Max and I would have long discussions. We would go to watch all kinds of matches together, especially in Germany. We didn't miss anything, from the warm-up to the end of the match. Sometimes we'd get back from these trips at four or five in the morning, but it was such a formative experience. I think Max was the first person to sense that I was going to be a coach. He offered me the position of coach at the training academy, and when he could have returned to the post himself after being removed from the first team, he didn't want it. 'It's your turn now,' he said.

I did everything at the training academy and I loved it. I was learning on the job. I massaged the players, I strapped them up, I met the parents, I organised the travel. I went to watch every training session I could, in order to learn. I read technical books to acquire the basics, all the know-how I didn't yet have, before going on to study at CREPS, the regional centre for sports education, and then earning my badge at the national football institute at Vichy.

Strasbourg was like a laboratory for me to try out all the things I would subsequently do as a coach. I was lucky enough to be trusted, given carte blanche in a way, at the training academy. I wanted to look for and to find new methods for giving the players what they needed. But there too I had my doubts. I was barely 30 and I was coaching young people of eighteen or nineteen. What should I teach them? I needed to be bold, and try everything for them. For example, I had a psychiatrist brought into the club for the first time. He met the players individually every week, to help them to assess their capacities, to face their fears. It was unheard of, and even today I'm not sure it's something many teams do.

Strasbourg was also where I started trying to develop the players' mental capacities. The expectation to perform puts players under pressure, and good players always need to be able to make a clear analysis of the game in order to choose an optimal solution.

Many men played a crucial role in the development of my coaching career.

At a regional level, there were the technical advisers, Jacky and Pierrot Demut, who schooled me in the basics. Pierrot and I had long animated conversations into the night at CREPS in Strasbourg.

There was Petrescu, a Romanian whom CREPS brought over to Strasbourg to teach us his training techniques, his art if you like. He helped me to advance my understanding of football apprenticeships and coaching. He was twenty years ahead of his time. He was already working on exercises for improving short- and long-term memory, and he had a perfect understanding of how players learn.

At a national level, there was Georges Boulogne, who did a lot for coaches. He devised training programmes and formalised the education of coaches; he fought club presidents to make them set up *centres de formation*. He had been a coach for the French team. He knew the job. And he knew how lonely it was, how thankless it could sometimes be. At the time, coaches could be fired from one day to the next with nothing to show for it. It was with him that I took my diploma to become a professional coach. And afterwards, we remained very close. He was often the person who told me after a lost title, a defeat, 'Sometimes you've just got to let other people have their turn,' and he was right, even if I always found that hard to accept.

Giving up my place as a player happened quite naturally. One day the Strasbourg president said to me: 'You're starting to get too old.' Stung, I didn't play, to the surprise of all the other players. I watched the match and . . . the players outdid themselves! I understood: it was time for me to concentrate wholly on being a coach.

Everything was a series of sequential, logical, deliberate progressions. I met so many wonderful people who were the gateway to better things for me. I seized the opportunities that came my way, and learnt how to make on-the-spot decisions.

Those years, all those experiences at those clubs and with those coaches I admired, have left me with some amazing memories and some terrible ones.

I remember in particular a match with Strasbourg in the 1978–79 season, the year of our French championship title. A one-on-one that I lost. We were playing Reims and I was opposite the Argentine winger Santiago Santamaría, an incredible player. He intercepted a ball, taking advantage of a mistake of mine, and we conceded a goal. It was my fault. I blamed myself so much. And to this day I remember how angry I was with myself, how guilty I felt. Of course there were all the goals scored, the victories, but among the moments that stand out, that mistake against Santamaría still stings.

Guilt, injustice, the violence of some matches too – it was still a time when referees looked the other way, when there was no TV broadcast, when we turned out the lights at the end of the matches, when there were violent ambushes between players – the anger we sometimes felt could be huge motivators.

Alongside these sometimes difficult feelings, it was also a time when I felt a huge admiration for the players I met and spent time with. The real stars of the day were Alfredo Di Stéfano, Pelé, Franz Beckenbauer and Günter Netzer. Netzer was a midfielder like me and a source of inspiration with his long passes and his ability to switch wings. I was also a big fan of Beckenbauer, who had such incredible elegance. He was an artist. We never played against each other, of course, but we did compete when he managed Marseille for a few months when I was at Monaco.

I also met Guy Roux when he was coach at Auxerre and I was playing for Mutzig, and I scored the deciding goal against him. Later on, even if our methods and personalities were very different, I respected what he did at Auxerre, the way he took his team into the European Cup, and the extraordinary longevity of his tenure (44 years!) at the club.

During all these years of my professional development, I admired the coaches. The ones who respected the players, the game, the beauty of the game, who made their team play first and foremost and who did not just count on their opponents' weakness. That was how it was with Max Hild, with Gilbert Gress and Johan Cruyff. To me, football can only call itself a profession if its aim is to make people dream. I understood this as I watched those men coach their teams.

And I had infinite respect for the players: the ones who had a philosophy of the game, who favoured individual expression, who were not afraid to fight and confront their fears, rather than submit to them.

Those were the reasons that I had for admiring people, and the things I looked for in all the players at my clubs.

Understanding the feelings that drive a player, his fear or his anger, admiring his art when it serves the game and the team, always respecting coaches, listening – I learnt and felt all this in those years. I was ready then to leave Alsace, my mentors, my friends, and to coach alone, to face new challenges.

'The coach's role is to make the player understand everything that serves the interests of the game. To do this, he must speak to the child within each player, to the adolescent he was and the adult he is now. Too often a coach tends only to speak to the adult, issuing commands for performance, for victory, for reflection, to the detriment of the child who is playing for pleasure, living in the present.'

3

CANNES AND NANCY:
MY FIRST YEARS
AS A COACH

RC Strasbourg was the passion of my youth. I had been the coach at the training academy, I'd spent all my time with the players. I tried to attend as many matches as I could in Alsace and in Germany. I read everything I could find about the art of coaching. I also created a school for children aged five to seven within the training centre. I had a freedom that allowed me to influence the life of the club, to work in any way I chose, always innovating. I could have stayed there for a long time, which is what my mentors, along with Racing's directors, were advising me to do: to keep working hard, with passion, climbing the rungs of the ladder and one day becoming the coach of the first team.

But a part of me wanted adventure more than comfort. I wanted to discover a new kind of football, new players, men with different coaching methods, to never stop making progress.

During a match that pitted my team against the Mulhouse reserve team, I met Jean-Marc Guillou. It was an encounter that proved crucial, just like those earlier ones with Max Hild and Georges Boulogne had been.

Jean-Marc had been a great player, first at Angers then at Nice. He was an incomparable attacking midfielder. He'd also played in the French national team, most notably in the 1978 World Cup in Argentina. He belonged to that generation of fabulous players who had been slightly for-gotten in favour of the generation that came after them, a generation who had been sacrificed, who had had to stay in a club for years, toiling away and accomplishing great things to get themselves noticed. I find this even more striking today because – and I don't mean to exaggerate – I sometimes get the impression that one match is now enough for a talented player to be discovered. After his career as a player, Jean-Marc Guillou had become the coach at Mulhouse, which he had led from the second division to the first.

After that match between our teams, Jean-Marc wanted to meet me. We talked for hours. Our close bond in work and friendship was formed instantly. Jean-Marc was – and still is – such a forceful character, with very precise ideas about the game that I admired and shared. When he became first-team coach at AS Cannes, who were then in the second division, he offered me the chance to become his assistant and coach of the training academy.

I took the decision to follow him without talking to anybody and without listening to those who were advising me to stay in Strasbourg. I went to Cannes to meet Jean-Marc Guillou and to be introduced to the club's general manager, Richard Conte, who later became a friend but whom I didn't know at the time. We talked and negotiated over the contract all night, and didn't reach an agreement until the small hours of the morning. The amounts we were arguing about would seem laughable today but nobody wanted to give way, and that's just what we were like: three men with strong personalities, who didn't want to lose, who didn't want to give ground, who were ready to fight. We would later make up an amazing trio: we never argued, we respected one another's positions, and we moved forward with the same ideas and the same love for the club.

That night's discussion is a particularly strong and intact memory. It sealed a cherished friendship, which still unites us today. It also marked the first time I left Alsace, the first steps I took as a coach, my first negotiations. Alone, determined, following my instincts, concerned to prove to others and to myself that I was up to the job, and anxious, too, but without allowing that anxiety to paralyse me.

I have retained another memory from that departure for AS Cannes which says a lot about my own state of mind and about what football was like at the time. I knew that Jean-Marc was looking to sign a centre-forward. Just before my departure, I read some impressive statistics in *France Football* on a player at SC Orange, Lamine N'Diaye. His results made him the best goalscorer. I called him before setting off by car for Cannes. I remember our conversation and my proposal to him almost word for word: a meeting with a few friends in a car park close to the motorway exit for Orange. 'I'll bring my boots. We're going to play football.' The next day, he was there. We played four-against-four and then one-on-one and I knew right away what a superb player he was, what potential he had. Jean-Marc Guillou, who had joined me and was watching everything, shared my enthusiasm. The following day, we took him to Cannes to sign his first professional contract. He was the first player I recruited for the team and he subsequently became a real friend. He played in Ligue 1 for a long time, first at Cannes, then at Mulhouse. Then he managed Coton Sport de Garoua in Cameroon, then the Senegal national team and had several successful seasons at Congolese club TP Mazembe. But I think that first meeting in the car park near Orange is something we both remember. Can you imagine somebody signing a player like that today?

*

I stayed just a year at AS Cannes as assistant coach and head of the training academy, but the year would be a decisive one.

It was a sizeable challenge. I rather had the impression, when I left Strasbourg for Cannes, that I was giving up a Rolls-Royce for a 2CV. It was as if I was agreeing to move down a level, but it was also exciting because we were in at the start of something, and the connection between Jean-Marc, Richard and me was perfect. AS Cannes was a club still in the making, in the second division, with no professional structure. Together with Richard and Jean-Marc, everything needed to be done: set up a training academy, recruit young people, carry out trials, restructure the team, rethink the training sessions. Giving ourselves to it almost 24/7. It was a really big job and I think that's why I liked it so much, why that year was so intense and formative.

Those first weeks in that city in the south of France I knew nobody but Jean-Marc and Richard, whereas in Strasbourg I'd had my whole family and my friends. It was a wrench to leave Alsace. I was living in real isolation. I had found an apartment where I was living like a total ascetic. There was just a bed, a sofa, and a TV so that every night I could watch over and over again the matches I'd recorded. But experiencing that loneliness so completely also helped me to understand the state of mind of a player who arrives at a club and in a town he doesn't know at all.

With that in mind, I have always allowed a player time – at least six months – to get his bearings, to feel at home, and to concentrate on the game.

Living that isolated, solitary life, where nothing was familiar, was a revelation. I learnt that I could live anywhere and be alone with my passion, with no interference, no personal affection, and that the anxieties did not disappear but I could live with them. That I was a solitary man who liked to be with the team, who liked the solitude of decision-making and preparation as much as the sharing of the pleasure in the game, the intensity of the match.

It was also hard at first to leave Alsatian football for a football with such a different technique and mentality. At Cannes and in the south of France generally, the game is more about footwork, while in Alsace it's longer, the average pass is longer, it's more about creating spaces. At Cannes, then, the game was shorter, with more footwork, more technical. And more violent. That was the other major difference: the roughness of the opposing teams, the intimidation of the referee and of the opposing side, which went hand in hand with seeming impunity and consequently made the coach feel powerless. I got used to it quickly, but I'd never known anything like it in Alsace. That discovery, too, was formative: for the young players, we needed to confront this head on, to show we weren't afraid, we were ready to respond, and I liked that nervousness, that passion, that tension.

*

Running the training academy together with my role as assistant coach of the first team meant a substantial workload. I sometimes found myself running four training sessions a day! The youngsters between 8:30 a.m. and 10, and 2 p.m. to 4, the first-team players from 10:15 to midday and 4 p.m. to 6. When the team travelled, I'd go with them, come back on Sunday morning, do the post-match warmdowns at the grounds and then sometimes set off again with the reserve team to play in Marseille, for example. It was a sustained pace of work that I imposed on myself and on others. That was a constant throughout my career: I was trusted, and I should say that with Jean-Marc Guillou the trust was mutual. I had great freedom in my work, and in exchange I behaved as if the club belonged to me. I could argue over my contract for hours – or even through a whole night – without letting a single thing go, but once that contract was signed, I gave my all. And most importantly, I never went back to renegotiate a contract to my benefit.

I was sure I would do justice to my position, and that I would earn the players' respect, by putting quality and perseverance into the training sessions, and always being available. At the time it was sheer hard work that made the difference, not financial clout. The aim was to form a team that could make it into the first division, and set up a high-quality training academy. All of us – president, coach, players – worked towards that goal. The prevailing atmosphere was of relentless work and simultaneously of a very pleasant family ambience. There was an amazing team spirit, the same fighting spirit, a shared desire to play, win and enjoy ourselves that I have always looked for and sometimes found in the clubs where I subsequently coached. When the match was over, we would eat together. The following morning, we would have our breakfast together, and talk about everything.

The group of players we had brought together and trained up was enthusiastic and mature. They weren't young but they had a will of steel: they wanted to succeed. There was of course Lamine N'Diaye in midfield, but also Jean Fernandez, Gilles Rampillon and Yves Bertucci, forwards like Patrick Revelli and Bernard Castellani, and in defence Gilles Eyquem, Baptiste Gentili and Bernard Casoni.

Cannes was where I learnt to understand players better and discovered that even starting off with practically nothing, with derisory means but a great deal of willpower, we could make progress and succeed. There have been other examples of small clubs succeeding, like Auxerre back in the day or Amiens now.

Cannes was also where I made my initial mistakes.

A coach, like a player, learns from the game on the pitch.

At first, Jean-Marc and I didn't know the team well, and we assessed each player's position wrongly. We were a team with a very strong attacking dynamic and an imbalance up front. We conceded too many goals. Jean-Marc was a great innovator. He wasn't afraid to take risks. In football, having a well-balanced team is essential and it takes time to find it, and sometimes that balance depends upon one single player. I learnt a lot at Jean-Marc's side. I understood that football should be structured around a balance between possession and progression. I realised that the attacking spirit should not be without a backup, that you ought to weigh up the risks and find a good compromise, that you needed an adequate number of holding midfielders to provide a solid base and an adequate number of creative players to add the flair to hurt the opposition. And I realised that I wanted to be one of those coaches, like Jean-Marc or Max Hild, who don't simply bet on the opposing team's weaknesses.

Before Cannes, at Strasbourg, at the training academy, I took a particular interest in developing players for the future. At Cannes, the aim was the present. We needed results quickly. Every decision became important and it didn't take long for the consequences to be seen. We were all about the short term. We put together a team and we had to find a harmony and a balance fast.

Often a change of position can make a player really start to soar. The coach's powers of observation play a crucial part here. More than any psychological tests, it's the game that really reveals men's personalities. There is no longer any social veneer. You become what you really are.

57

At Cannes, Jean-Marc and I possibly made another mistake that we subsequently learnt to avoid. At the start of the season, we set off with the team to spend three weeks at Saint-Martin-Vésubie, and we 'exhausted' the players by training them too hard. We had scheduled three training sessions per day, and running in the mountains every morning. Some players went to bed at 8 p.m. but told me quite seriously that they couldn't get to sleep: they were dreading the following day too much.

The players started off lacking energy. And it took them time to recover. Later, we kept on training hard but we reduced the pace and gained in accuracy, in quality. I still believe that working through the pain during training makes it possible to bear it during matches, but I also understood the downsides of a training schedule that is too heavy, which can take its toll at the start of the season.

The other big lesson from Cannes was that I was able to be on the front line and coach the pros. And I liked it. Jean-Marc Guillou went off to the Ivory Coast for a few weeks to recruit an exciting forward I would later meet again at AS Monaco: Youssouf Fofana, a spectacular player with unbelievable power and explosiveness. Suddenly, without Jean-Marc, I was faced with the real problems a coach has to deal with: I put the team together on my own, I travelled with the team, took responsibility for the result. I liked that responsibility, I liked that constant tension, I liked that power. That experience of having sole control in

Cannes was really the moment when it became obvious to me that I wanted this much-coveted role, and confirmed my ambitions.

The season ended with a Coupe de France quarter-final loss to Monaco. But earlier in the competition, we had knocked out Bastia, who were a fine team, and most importantly we had started to feel like we were on the rise, becoming confident, gaining in strength. The club, we sensed, had a future. Later, with players who were more experienced, like Alain Moizan, Albert Emon, Félix Lacuesta and Daniel Sanchez, the club would reach the first division with Jean Fernandez and Richard Conte at the helm. And then the training academy we created became home to exceptional players like Zinedine Zidane, Patrick Vieira and Johan Micoud.

At the end of that year, I received offers from FC Sochaux-Montbéliard and AS Nancy. I immediately discussed the situation with Jean-Marc, who encouraged me, advising me to go for Nancy. They were the more insistent of the two, and there was also Aldo Platini as director of football, and he and I liked each other a lot. I had met the club president already. I'd made my decision. I was leaving Cannes for Nancy. I was signing my first pro contract in Ligue 1.

At the age of 34, at Nancy, I was becoming coach of the first team. And I was moving up a level, taking charge of a first-division club. I was entering another world with up-and-coming coaches like Aimé Jacquet, Jean-Claude Suaudeau, Gérard Houllier, Daniel Jeandupeux, who would all go on to great careers, and Guy Roux who was already well established at Auxerre. This was a world where I was really going to be tested and where I would have to prove myself. Some of the players were experienced men who looked at me at first with a sort of suspicion, a sort of reserve: Eric Martin, Ruben Umpierrez, Bruno Germain, Didier Casini, Didier Philippe, Albert Cartier. I had Jean-Luc Arribart brought over from Reims – an excellent player. It was a strong team, with experience, but at a club that had no money. There was a visionary president, Claude Cuny, who had transformed AS Nancy into a professional club, and equipped it with good-quality structures and a training academy. The team had had a superb captain, Michel Platini, and had known great victories like the Coupe de France against Nice in 1978. Platini, an extraordinary player, one of the great stars of the 1980s, would go on to lead the French team, and I would like to pay tribute to that generation who restored confidence to French football and who brought France its long-overdue international success, bringing home a first European Championship title in 1984. Every great French football triumph subsequently was built on that one.

Nancy was a big challenge for me as a young coach, and also a proper schooling: we'd have to balance the budget, live frugally, do what we could with whatever we had against better-financed clubs like Metz and Bordeaux, cities that were more football-oriented and with a larger fanbase.

I was clearly on the front line. Those were three thrilling years – difficult at times, but very formative. On this adventure, I could rely on a director of football, Aldo Platini, Michel's father, who had a great eye, who gave fascinating assessments, and with whom I talked a lot – and directors who, as at Cannes and at the other clubs where I would coach, would give me a free hand. In spite of the lack of means, I was able to progress in my own fashion, learning, putting my methods in place, innovating.

I was also focused on all the things that contribute to performance besides training: dietary regimes, massage, mental preparation, sleep, quality of life, the people the players had around them. A player must live in a state of constant preparation. I'd already started thinking about this a great deal in Alsace, particularly with Pierrot Demut. A player would do all his training, and then outside the club all those benefits would be lost. But a player should consider everything and get himself in shape to achieve the finest performance he can. What really matters is the progress made by the player.

'Invisible' training – that is, a holistic approach to fitness and lifestyle, including nutrition, sleep, stretching, massage, etc., as well as psychological support and motivation – is a part of what makes this progress possible. It was an innovation. The way a player approaches his training is decisive. You have to train to win. By the time they're five years into their careers, there is a huge gulf between the player who trains with great determination to progress and the one who is satisfied with his standard.

It was at Nancy – with that team of experienced players in the first year, and then in the second and third years with younger players who had come out of the training academy run by Alain Perrin, a future coach of the club – that I was better able to observe the players and get an understanding of the fundamental mechanics of attack, of defence, of fear. Many coaches come into the job without having been players and without having spent time in *centres de formation* where everyone from the youngest children from the age of five to teenagers of 15–17 is developed. I was lucky to have had experience of these centres at Strasbourg and then at Cannes, and as a coach I still had an interest in training and development, in the stages that make it possible for players first to acquire technique (between 7 and 12) and then to develop physically (between 12 and 16), then to deepen their mental resilience (between 17 and 19) and finally between 19 and 22 to acquire what is critical, like the roof of a house without which all the rest rots away: intelligence and motivation. It is a long-term job. During those three years at Nancy, then even more so at Monaco and at Arsenal, I knew that was what really mattered the most.

The player grows up, goes through all these stages, and places himself at the service of the game. That should be his only religion. Serving the interests of the game, taking the optimal decision in each situation he's faced with. Even if this means sometimes going against individual temptation. A player cannot understand this all at once. He needs time: to receive the ball, to battle against his opponent, to weigh up the risk of losing the ball, and come to his decision. The coach's role is to make the player understand everything that serves the interests of the game. To do this, he must speak to the child within each player, to the adolescent he was and the adult he is now. Too often a coach tends only to speak to the adult, issuing commands for performance, for victory, for reflection, to the detriment of the child who is playing for pleasure, living in the present.

I have always tried to protect my players from stressful environments and to make them live in the moment of the game, free of any threat of judgement and fear of consequences.

Often when a young coach comes to see me to ask for advice, I tell them to imprint their vision of the game, and not to forget that the game itself is also a good coach and that observation is often as effective as talking.

During a match there are billions of possible combinations, and that's what makes football the wonderful, rich, surprising sport that it is. A player is constantly adapting his technique to the situation. He cannot act just on reflex. He has to prepare, correct himself, find his place, decide: all this is something he acquires, he works on, he builds on, but he will need to be innovating constantly as he makes his decisions because the situation will never be exactly the same as whatever he experienced in the previous scenario, in the previous match. Our sport depends on three criteria: ball control, decision-making and the quality of execution.

A coach should instil in his team a respect for the game, a feeling for the group. Everywhere I've coached, there were some players who were a bit lax with that rule. It is down to the coach to persuade them that what they put into the team, the team will give back to them. But the higher the level, the more the competition intensifies, the more these players are a handicap to the team. I have always, from Nancy to Arsenal, sought out players who do not cheat when it comes to their commitment to others.

It was at Nancy that that search really took on a central role. My life is so associated with Arsenal today that people have rather forgotten how formative my experiences coaching those first teams were. For what they gave me, what they taught me.

Once I started at Nancy, I committed myself totally to the club for those three years. And I managed to win players over by being committed, by being demanding, even severe, too, sometimes. I waged a bit of a war on the rebels. I wanted involvement from everybody that was equal to mine and up to the standards of the game. That was crucial for me. I felt that my career as a coach was at stake and that there was everything to play for. That was when I started keeping an eye on absolutely everything, to become a manager in the fullest sense of the word, to decide as many things as possible.

I knew the club wasn't rich compared to other Ligue 1 clubs that had more significant municipal grants, more supporters, and could also count on the takings from the European cups. I was as careful with the money as the club president. And so I would sometimes drive alone to Munich where the ISPO sporting goods and services trade fair was held, and go – all of this on my own – from stand to stand to negotiate the purchase of footballs for the club: for example, once reaching a deal with Derby who would supply me with 100 balls per season at a reasonable price. I returned to Nancy proud of my business deal, happy for the club.

I gradually came to understand that if I wanted the best possible conditions – like the best possible footballs – even the tiniest detail was important. That was why I would talk to the groundsmen every morning, and hassle them about improving the state of the turf, and why I gave less expensive younger players a chance when the team's star players started to move on.

As I was very involved and on the front line for the first time, I experienced intense joys, especially that initial year with some great matches and fine victories, but also for the first time I really suffered as a result of my passion. I was always with the team. I took responsibility for my choices. I knew that I must deal with the disappointment of the player who was not selected on the Friday and the risk he might not forgive me, and that I needed to get his confidence and motivation back on Monday. Most of all I accepted that only I could take responsibility for defeat. I understood how intolerable defeat was to me – actually physically unbearable. In the second and third years, the level of the team slipped, everything was more difficult, and the defeats more numerous. I learnt to live with the suffering of defeat and I discovered that football, to me, was a matter of life and death.

We lost one match, for example, on the eve of the Christmas break. I didn't go out for days – only on Christmas Eve to visit my parents – and dragged myself around like a poor wretch, a zombie. Today I'm a little ashamed of my uncompromising nature, and I still don't know why I took defeat so badly, but I know that that pain, that dark place within me, was also the place where I learnt patience, endurance and rigour: I needed each time to rediscover the resources to motivate the others while I myself was at my worst and hiding whatever I might feel. I spent the Christmas break alone at my place because I knew no one would notice. I could allow myself this isolation; the players were on holiday and, as soon as this dark period was over, I knew

I would regain my optimism. I lived alone with that pain and the reflections that accompanied it for three weeks, and looking back I realise now that it was a kind of vaccine against everything that would happen later.

Another incident in my life explains this capacity to live with pain without it denting my confidence in the future, my certainty that after all the defeats, a victory is possible. At the age of fourteen, I spent several days hovering between life and death, struck by a terrible fever nobody could explain. But one day the fever broke and life regained the upper hand. I remember – and my body remembers, too – how I suffered in those days. I was not very tall at that age, just four foot seven. And mysteriously I grew very fast after that. At seventeen, I was five foot eleven. It was a lesson: never to lose hope, never to give yourself up for lost.

After that, I came to believe that I could survive anything.

I quickly understood at Nancy that those years were sometimes going to be difficult. The first year, after three matches we were at the top of the table with Bordeaux. We faced them and we lost to a goal by Alain Giresse. That defeat marked me, too: it was like a turning-point. Even if we had started off well, Bordeaux and others were better than us, and we were going to have to fight. The second year we managed to stay in Ligue 1, and the third year we kept on believing right up until the final match of the season. By good fortune, we were surrounded by directors who trusted me and who, even at the moment of relegation, offered me a new five-year contract. I was ready to stay, to coach the club and enable it to get back up into Ligue 1. I gave it a lot of thought. At the same time, I had received offers from Francis Borelli at Paris Saint-Germain (PSG) and Jean-Louis Campora at Monaco. I met everybody. It was Richard Conte, the general manager of AS Cannes, who persuaded me to choose Monaco.

'Passing the ball is communicating with another person, it's being in the service of another person . . . For the pass to be a good one, the player has to put himself in the position of the person who's going to receive it.'

4

MONACO

When I was working at AS Cannes with Jean-Marc Guillou and Richard Conte, I had got a sense of the aura, the appeal that Monaco had. It was a first-division club that represented the Principality, and Prince Rainier himself followed the club's fortunes closely. The family was and still is very attached to the sport, and Prince Albert is very passionate about it. Jean-Louis Campora, whom I'd met on several occasions, had led the club since 1975.

At just 37, I was young to be coaching a club like that, but I had the ambition, and clear ideas about what I wanted. Monaco could offer me and the players optimal living and training conditions. And that was why I had chosen them rather than staying at Nancy or moving to PSG.

Jean-Louis had chosen me over other coaches, but I needed to rise to the challenge, to prove myself. That team of men, those sturdy and experienced lads, were all wondering who this unknown Alsatian was, who had come from a club that had been relegated, was barely older than they were and seemed rather strict and cold. I would need to show them I could live up to the club's ambitions.

President Campora had incidentally kept the former coach Ştefan Kovács in the club, to advise him but also, I imagine, as a stand-in if I turned out not to be up to the standard required. From the start, I was being monitored. Just like those players who arrive in a team and who, sooner or later, need to make their presence felt on the pitch and in the dressing room, I needed to impose my values, my demands, my philosophy of the game. So I kept my distance from Kovács in order to be freer, and I started working with Jeannot Petit, who became my assistant. He too was already there when I arrived, and he was well acquainted with the club and top-level sport. It's important for a manager to have an assistant who knows the club's culture well. Jeannot had been a player for years. I could also count on Henri Biancheri, the technical director, who was another former Monaco player. We got along very well and bit by bit, as a result of hard work, of always being around and because the opening league matches of the season went well, the doubts and the reservations disappeared.

Coming from a lower-ranked team, and having, earlier in my career, known numerous defeats, more modest clubs, difficult moments, inferior conditions, all this gave me an invaluable humility. This helped me keep a cool head when we had amazing results that first year, and equally not to despair when the going became tough and the climate unhealthy.

It was that mixture of ambition and humility, that balance, that I had within me and that defined me when I arrived at Monaco.

Before the season started, we were looking for a number 10. The president had given me the choice of Glenn Hoddle, the England playmaker, who was at the end of his contract with Tottenham Hotspur and was being courted by PSG, and another player who operated more on the wing: Marko Mlinarić, another skilful footballer, who was at Dinamo Zagreb. Jean-Louis Campora had asked me to take a quick trip from Monaco to Zagreb to see him play and make a decision. When I got back, at midnight, Campora's daughter was waiting for me at Nice airport. She told me I needed to decide the following morning at six. I remember returning home and spending the whole night watching tapes of the matches, asking myself a whole heap of questions, certain that one of the two players would be decisive for the team.

At 5:30, I called Glenn Hoddle's agent: he and Glenn were already at the airport, getting ready to head to Paris to join PSG. I told them to get on a plane, but one headed for Monaco. We needed a creative player, and in the matches I'd watched, Glenn delivered some amazing balls. And besides, a few weeks earlier we had just recruited another Englishman as a striker, Mark Hateley, and I knew the two of them would get along well. Glenn was to become a legend at Monaco. The other players in the team rated him, and the fans still consider him the player of the century.

My first year in Monaco, 1988, was like a footballing dream. I found an apartment in Villefranche in the same building as Richard Conte. Every day I would go to the club, in La Turbie, to meet the players; I was interested only in them and in the next match. I had a few friends I would see on occasional evenings and with whom of course I talked football, or we'd watch matches: Richard Conte and Jean-Marc Guillou, obviously, but also the Cannes artist Peritza, Boro Primorac who played at Cannes and whom I liked very much, Bernard Massini, and Roland Scheubel. It was a group of friends who knew I was obsessed by my passion and who understood and supported me.

The club, the players and I all had huge challenges to overcome: Monaco hadn't yet got past the first round of the European Cup, and hadn't been French champions in years. We all wanted the club to carve out a place for itself at the highest level.

To make this happen, we could depend upon the ambition of Campora, who knew football very well and who was a good friend of Jean Sadoul, president of the French football league. Campora was a winner, and almost as bad a loser as I was. He had built an amazing training academy and I had a really good relationship with Pierre Tournier, the coach there, and with the man who looked after the youngsters, Paul Pietri.

We could also depend upon a dream team with some really good players. Some of them had been trained by Gérard Banide, between 1979 and 1983, robust men, well established in the team, like Manuel Amoros, the best left-back in the world; Claude Puel; our goalkeeper Jean-Luc Ettori, a very strong influence at AS Monaco; Dominique Bijotat; Bruno Bellone; Luc Sonor . . . These players showed huge confidence on the pitch: they knew what they wanted, they didn't let themselves be pushed around. I could sense this immediately in the training sessions and during the opening matches. Their charisma was connected to their knowledge and experience. When things were difficult, they kept their self-control. And then they were great professionals who also enjoyed the good things in life, a spirit that has been lost in more recent times. It was a generation who were starting to earn a good living for themselves but who hadn't forgotten they'd had to make it there the hard way. They discussed everything, showing respect for the coach but giving their own opinions, too. It was possible for us to talk. They were not yet surrounded by lawyers, agents, advisers who are really family members, all those middlemen who would gradually get between a player and his coach.

They all considered themselves Monégasques, local men, ready to fight for the city, for the club, and they were perfect incarnations of the spirit of Monaco: that mixture of pride and ambition, that quest for excellence, that rejection of mediocrity. All those of us who worked for the Principality felt the same way. We had to represent it as best we could, to be up to scratch, to have respect for rituals, and I liked that, and I liked the way that, at the time, that spirit influenced the game and the behaviour of the men on the pitch.

When I think about the difference between life in Monaco and life in my village, it makes my head spin.

The first match was important. It was a real test. We were playing Marseille, who after Bordeaux would become our main rivals. They had star players like the striker Jean-Pierre Papin. We were less sure of ourselves. The team was good but how good was it against a team that was at the very top of the championship? Were we a middle-of-the-table team or a top-of-the-table team?

We built an unassailable lead in the first half and went on to win 3-1. That match was decisive: it gave hope to the whole team and it gave the players some confidence in me. In the next match, we travelled to Lens, and there, too, we made a great impression, winning again. After six matches we had continued to perform strongly, losing only once, to Montpellier. The seventh game was much harder. We were at home to Niort. And we lost. President Campora was invaluable here. It was one of the rare occasions when he spoke to the players. He gave me a huge helping hand at a delicate moment when I didn't yet have complete sway over the team, when I was still in a trial phase. He gave them a quiet little talk. Thanks to that, the players didn't lose their faith in themselves. Nor in me. I'm convinced the success of that year and the league title hinged on that moment.

Gradually I was able to show my values, my convictions, and share them with my assistants and the team. I was very demanding in training. I was very vocal. I'm sure some of them will remember my shouting and our arguments. I had no tolerance for poor passing or lack of willpower. I admit I was sometimes unfair, but since I was facing strong personalities who didn't hesitate to say what they thought, I think those rages boosted the energy levels. It was only later that I became more tolerant.

I was also in great physical shape: I worked hard, I led from the front, and that had an impact on the players. When we went away to a training camp for ten days, we trained three times a day. And then I imposed very strict pre-match dietary regimens. Every action we took needed to contribute so that we were in the best possible condition for the matches lying ahead of us. I wanted the best masseurs for my players, the best osteopaths. Everything mattered, including and especially the state of the grass! The groundsmen at Monaco must have popped the champagne when I left! The stadium had been built on top of a car park. There was 40cm of earth laid down on top of concrete. But the summer with its high temperatures, the salt, the sea air, it was all terrible for the grass and for us: it left the turf rough and bumpy which interfered with our passing game. We would stretch out covers to protect it from the sun and we had to remove them again every night. Sometimes the covers weren't well placed or weren't put on at all; the groundsmen would hear about it from me then!

As I said earlier, Pierrot Demut and I had talked a lot at Strasbourg about 'invisible' training, about the importance of dietary regimens. I wanted my players to be able to fully express themselves while taking all that into account. And naturally I had to embody those same values myself: at training sessions, in exercises, when we were having lunch, whenever we travelled. Apart from cigarettes. I'd started smoking while I watched football videos at night when I was assistant coach at Cannes. At Monaco, I smoked all the time – you can find photos of me on the bench with a cigarette. But I'm getting ahead of myself. It was partly thanks to a cigarette that I would later be recruited to coach Arsenal! But I've always tried to stick to the principle that a leader should above all embody the values that he promotes.

As for any team, I tried to find the perfect position for each player, to allow them to express themselves, and to be attacking, to play some attractive football. I had my intermediaries in the team, strong men with experience I could count on, like goalkeeper Jean-Luc Ettori, and defenders Manuel Amoros, Patrick Battiston and Luc Sonor. That was one of the lessons from Monaco: if the coach has a good bond with the best players, that makes him stronger. If not, he'll be swimming against the current. It's thanks to his players and thanks to his convictions that a whole team can adopt these same values, share them and move forwards together.

Another player I was able to lean on was Glenn Hoddle, who wasn't a long-standing member of the team but whose results had earned him everybody's respect. He was one of the few players I've known to have a religious faith: he would read the Bible whenever we were travelling. And on the pitch he was a magician. I liked Claude Puel's determination, too. Sometimes I didn't play him, but he understood. I wanted him to think about what kind of player he was. And it did him no harm as he was certain of his strength and was an amazing fighter, totally determined. Even in training sessions he always wanted to win. He never let up on an opponent. Luc Sonor, meanwhile, had an amazing capacity for speed and dribbling. I repositioned him and played him down the side. And I organised private sessions for him: I made him watch matches and I put specific training sessions in place – I got him crossing a lot, for example. I put similar sessions and one-to-one work in place for others, too. Each player had to work on the qualities they needed in their position.

We quickly chose zonal marking, at a time when everybody else was marking man-to-man. Patrick Battiston and Rémi Vogel were doing it already, and after the arrival of Roger Mendy we extended this practice to the rest of the team.

In training sessions at Monaco we emphasised technical abilities above everything. Passing the ball is communicating with another person, it's being in the service of another person. It's crucial. For the pass to be a good one, the player has to put himself in the position of the person who's going to receive it. It's an act of intelligence and generosity. What I call technical empathy.

Training allowed me to develop the players' ability to express themselves on an individual and a collective level. I was aware of each one's troubles and how much they had fought to reach the top level, but I also had very high expectations where they were concerned.

A coach has to be both emotionally engaged and cool in

his decision-making. For him to be credible, he must have total control over the choice of the team. If a player thinks that an assistant or the club president can influence the coach's decision, that coach loses all credibility.

He should keep two-way communication permanently open. A coach tends to over-estimate the effectiveness of his communication. So there are some rules that need to be taken into account:

- On average two-thirds of people would do more if their qualities were better recognised.
- Less than 30 per cent of people apply the recommendations they've been given owing to a lack of confidence, a lack of respect for the coach or a lack of clarity or of practical recommendations. It's important to be clear in one's recommendations in order to boost confidence and improve performance.
- When expressing a negative point, one should put forward three positive points when speaking to a player or to somebody who needs to develop.
- One should not aim for multiple objectives: just one or two are enough.
- And never forget that time and place are very important.

Becoming a footballer is undoubtedly the most difficult of ambitions, but it is also the one in which you run the greatest risk of slipping into a comfort zone. Why? Because it's a team game in which individual players can hide. Because the salaries are such that there's nothing pushing them to continue progressing. Because no one in their entourage judges their performance with the proper rigour – on the contrary, everybody flatters them. How many good players then stagnate? To me, the whole point of training is to attain a high technical and mental level, because it's that level, which has long been neglected, that makes it possible to progress.

The coach should also promote collective expression by creating the conditions to allow the team to take risks, and encouraging them to do so. And when faced with a defeat, he should keep on going, stand firm, believe in his convictions, above all not blame the players. When he is preparing for a match, the coach's challenge is to succeed in destroying the opponent's strong points without preventing his own team from expressing themselves. If you exaggerate the opposition's qualities, you increase your players' fear and the risk that they will hide away. At Monaco, our strength, which was also related to the personality of the players, was that they did not hide: they weren't afraid of anybody.

Monaco was where I sensed so strongly that the coach creates a style and conveys it to his team, which comes through in the players' attitude and leaves its mark on them. The Monégasque style was all about positive expressions of the game and of the team's qualities. The coach's goal is to win and to fashion a playing style. That style is a team that expresses itself, that builds, that takes risks, that respects the collective game. It's satisfying to see your former players who have now become coaches sharing this vision of the game, though of course with different personalities.

At the end of that first year, the league title was ours. I still remember defeats more than victories, but a coach can never forget the first title he brings home. Before that, I knew I could get a team to win matches, but a league title is something else. It meant winning matches for a whole season and being in first place when it mattered. It gave me so much confidence, without ever making me forget where I'd come from.

And it also allowed me, while still remaining very focused on my work with the team, to spend more time at the training centre, to work even more closely with Pierre Tournier, the coach, to watch a lot of matches and try to unearth young talent. At Monaco we formed a real team of directors and coach, with huge solidarity in all areas including recruitment.

That was how I came to spot a player who would become exceptional: George Weah.

Claude Le Roy was the coach for Cameroon. He came to see me in Monaco. I confided in him, over lunch, that I had a concern about Mark Hateley getting injured so often. I was looking for a striker who might stand in for him. He immediately told me about a player at Tonnerre Yaoundé. When Claude got back to Cameroon, I would call him every Monday for several weeks and ask him for news about his promising striker. I sent Henri Biancheri to watch him play. He called me after the match. George had played with his hand in plaster, with a fracture. He hadn't done a lot, Henri told me, but when he received the ball the crowd had responded enthusiastically and that was a good sign. I brought him over. He was 23 years old. At his first training session, he made a pitiful impression: he wasn't physically ready at all. Everyone thought him hopeless, clumsy. He only spoke English and was very shy. It could only be him and me at first. Because when a coach chooses a man and gives him his debut, a very special relationship is established. He has to work hard to convince others and sometimes the player himself. And that work becomes a lesson in the art of stubbornness.

George worked incredibly hard. I took him running, we exercised together, just the two of us. Training makes men grow, and with him I could feel it at once; he gradually earned the respect of the others. He was slender but made of solid stuff. He developed a technical finesse, an artistry that nobody would have expected of him. He was smart, powerful, and match after match he gained in confidence. At first he used to get himself slaughtered in the penalty area and he said nothing. He just took it, he was amazing. I used to tell him, 'Come on, you can stay down, it's a penalty,' but no, he would get back up on his feet. He was a man of absolute honesty, focused completely on the game. He was a part of the team for the 1988–89 season. I had him play against Valur of Reykjavik, he scored and we qualified for the European Cup second round. And bit by bit, when he was paired up with Glenn Hoddle, he became a real star, one of the best players in the world. He was very alone to begin with, then season after season I brought over other Liberian players like the centre-forward James Debbah in 1991 and the attacking midfielder Kelvin Sebwe in 1992. They formed a close-knit group, which was invaluable.

But to see him when he arrived and started out in 1988, who would have predicted he would end up winning the Ballon d'Or in 1995? He was a miracle. No one could have predicted he would go on to do what he did. After us, he signed with PSG, then AC Milan, eventually ending his playing career at Marseille and in Abu Dhabi. I happened by chance to be in Milan when he was presented with the Ballon d'Or. He found out that I was around, and suggested I attend the ceremony. I had no official invitation and the security guards didn't want to allow me in. George had to intervene. I can only imagine the expressions on the faces of those suspicious guards when I came back out after the ceremony with the Ballon d'Or trophy that Weah had given me! It's a wonderful memory. Perhaps the only time a player has brought a coach onstage, handing him his award.

*

In that year, 1989, my second at Monaco, the tussle with Marseille was even tougher and it was they who were crowned champions. Marseille quickly became for us what Manchester United would become for Arsenal. They were a really talented team, with the best French players, with great passion and commitment. Just like their fans. And I absolutely loved those confrontations, that tension during the match: it really was us or them! We won often, and so did they, and that year they won the league, but we were always battling for first place. This was also the year we at last made an impression on the European Cup stage. Having got past the Icelanders Valur in the first round, we were faced with a second-round match against Club Brugge which we won 6-1 at home. A wonderful memory, but one that was followed by a quarter-final tie played in peculiar circumstances against Galatasaray. Following crowd trouble in the previous round the Turkish side were forced to play their home leg in Cologne in front of 70,000 fervent supporters, most of them from the city's large Turkish community. Ironically their home ground had only half that capacity, so UEFA's punishment rather backfired. I took this defeat particularly badly.

The following year, we had to keep going and put that defeat behind us, to keep fighting, to strengthen the team still further, to keep it moving forwards, and continue to

'Arsène before Arsenal': a *L'Équipe* magazine article that
covered my childhood and playing career.

My mother and father, Louise and Alphonse

Above With my parents, and my older sister and brother

Right At a wedding in Duttlenheim. In front of me is my cousin Martine.

My first football team in Duttlenheim. My father is on
the far left with his overcoat and hat. I am in the back
row – the second boy from the right.

Playing for Vauban in 1976. I am fourth from the left in the back row.

At the *centre de formation* (training academy) in Strasbourg
where I was a player and coach.

Above Playing for Vauban against Nice in the Coupe de France. My opponent is Roger Jouve.

Left and below At Racing Club de Strasbourg

UN ATOUT DE TAILLE DANS LE JEU DU FCM
ARSENE WENGER,
«UN GRAND BLOND AVEC...»

En annonçant, hier, que le FCM était en passe d'obtenir la signature d'un grand espoire du football alsacien, c'est bien

On my arrival at Monaco with the new recruits (from left to right): Mark Hateley, Glenn Hoddle, Rémy Vogel, Fabrice Mège and Patrick Battiston.

With George Weah, Ballon d'Or winner and future President of Liberia

Above Monaco winning the Coupe de France against Olympique de Marseille in 1991.

Left 'Monaco: the headache for Wenger'

MONACO :
LE CASSE-TÊTE
DE WENGER

find new young talent. After Weah, I found Lilian Thuram. He was a part of the same category of players, the miraculous ones, but in a quite different way from George Weah.

He was playing at CS Fontainebleau. He was a right midfielder. The coach of the Monaco junior team had brought him to my notice. The club president was a friend of mine. I called him for confirmation of this player's potential, which he gave me, but he informed me that he'd just signed an agreement with Nice. We went for broke: I sent a man to get him to sign another agreement, telling him to post it at once so that it would arrive at La Ligue first. The man from Nice who'd got Thuram to sign the first contract didn't post his letter until Monday. And so Lilian was able to come to Monaco.

He was a midfielder, but I switched him to a central defensive role because he was very good in aerial duels, was afraid of nobody and had amazing psychological strength. It was in the technical and tactical sphere that he had to be brought up to the highest level. He didn't have a defender's reflexes, but he had a terrific hunger to learn. I didn't have him play straight away. I wanted him first to work on his kicking. It was during one of those training sessions that he got injured. The doctor was concerned. The injury revealed a serious problem with his kneecap: the muscle wasn't properly aligned on the kneecap, as a result of which the muscle path was longer and, when he struck a ball hard, the muscle gave way. And he had that problem in both his legs. The doctor wanted to operate at once on both knees but we opted for just one operation: rehab would have been impossible if both had been immobilised. After the operation, he was away for a year. But bit by bit, thanks to that will of iron he had, he came back. He trained, he played and he never had that second knee operation. That was the miracle. If somebody had told me then that he was going to break the record for the most capped player in the French national team, and that he would score two goals at the World Cup, I would have thought they were crazy!

That was another lesson in stubbornness and modesty. In football, as in life, you should never close the door. I had faith in him, I believed in his enormous thirst to learn. It also fell to me to remove him from the team when he made huge mistakes, when he was over-precise, notably during one match against Metz. But he is the perfect example of a man with a natural solidity, who is totally committed to the fight, who seeks to understand his mistakes. To start off with, he wasn't at the same level as some of the other players, and he didn't have the technical capacities that he acquired over time. But he gradually raised his game to the very highest level.

The team and I continued to vie with Marseille and PSG in the 1989–90 season, finishing third in the championship. Then the following year we landed our second trophy, the Coupe de France. In Europe our steady improvement continued and we found that we were able to compete against the best teams, reaching the final of the 1992 Cup Winners' Cup.

We won, we progressed, we raised the club up and kept it at the top level with that generation of more experienced players I've already mentioned, with new recruits Weah and Thuram, and with the arrival of a new generation who had come out of the training academy at Monaco or other clubs. Among the men who came from the training academy was Emmanuel Petit, of course. He got slightly sidelined. People didn't quite trust him, they said he was a rebel, they didn't know if we should keep him. I wanted to trust him, like the time he got back the night before an important match at two in the morning. He had claimed it was the pressure, the tension of the match meant he couldn't sleep and needed to go for a walk, and I chose to believe him. And play him. He was very good. Sometimes careers are determined by tiny things. During a match he would give the team everything. Together with his extraordinary mental resources to keep fighting, including against his own insecurity, he had a real group generosity and great stamina. All the men who played with him knew just how good he was.

I also launched Youri Djorkaeff, who was playing at Strasbourg in the second division. My Alsatian friends had told me he was good, and Jeannot Petit, who went to watch him play, gave me confirmation of that. He did very well at

Monaco. He was sometimes over-reliant on his talent, but being intelligent, he also knew when he needed to give his all.

In order to keep making progress we used our training methods, our intensive, all-round preparation, and optimal structures and setting. We also made a lot of use – and were the first to do so – of a clever method of evaluation developed by my friend Jean-Marc Guillou.

Top Score is a tool for evaluating players based on observing and quantifying their performances. You assign points for each action the player carries out – for example, ten points for a forward pass, five for a sideways pass, two for a back pass – and you establish a defensive score and an offensive score which you add up.

At first, Jean-Marc found it hard to sell. We had talked about it day and night, and I'd followed its development. I thought the tool was excellent, as was anything that allowed for an objective evaluation of a player's performance. Until then, we had been relying on the subjectivity of the coach, and that wasn't enough. Everything we did was based on our own judgement, our own intuition. It was important for me to have the data to support me. I wanted an evaluation of a player's technical capacity through the quality of his passes, and his ball recovery. We wanted to measure the technical and tactical performance of individual players. Later, in England, I was the first manager to try and measure players' physical performance levels. I signed a contract with a company, who then sold this evaluation technique to ProZone and I entered into a contract with ProZone. We bought Stat DNA in 2011 to measure players' technical and tactical performance. We had had a contract with ProZone since the 2002–03 season to measure players' physical performance. They were two different aspects of evaluation.

At Monaco, I kept the results and I could follow a player's progress, his development. Thanks to Top Score, we realised that at the age of 32 a midfielder had a defensive score that was going down but an offensive score that was rising, that he had less energy to go into battle but more to express himself, to be more tactical. Rationality makes it possible to better understand the world around us.

A coach can't see everything. And sometimes, because he's disappointed, because his resentment or his anger gets the upper hand, he is not as objective as he might be. He is too close to his emotions. That was why I watched matches several times over. Top Score was an additional tool for gaining objectivity. President Campora, Jeannot Petit and I also realised what an opportunity Top Score represented on the transfer market. We knew Monaco had less money than PSG and Marseille or some of the big European clubs. We managed our finances sensibly, unlike those clubs that had taken on a whole new financial dimension. We needed to buy players but at a price we could afford, and we needed to find cheaper solutions. With the Top Score indicators we could buy players who had not yet been spotted and courted by other clubs. This also allowed us to give our own young players from the training academy their chance.

The following year, 1992, stood out for Monaco's great run in the Cup Winners' Cup and that terrible defeat in the final. We had got there without losing a match. Claude Puel was invaluable to the team, giving it defensive balance, but sadly he was injured in training so I put together a more offensive set-up, which was therefore more vulnerable when faced with a very good Werder Bremen side. But what changed everything in the final, and our spirits and our memories in the longer term, was the Furiani tragedy, which had happened the night before. During a Coupe de France semi-final between Bastia and Marseille in Corsica, terracing collapsed causing multiple deaths and injuries to spectators. At our hotel in Lisbon where the final was being held, we were left the whole night wondering whether the match would go ahead. How were we to play after what had happened? We played badly, the stadium was empty, our minds were elsewhere, and that defeat connected to our sadness scarred us all for life. The next day we accompanied President Campora to the hospital and the church in Bastia. Bastia was a club that did so much with such limited means. There was great emotion, and anger. We were all marked by it, like after the Heysel disaster in 1985.

At times like those, we felt so far away from the egotistical universe of competition. Eventually we immersed ourselves back in it, but without forgetting the dead and injured and the bereaved, and ensuring at our level, in the clubs and at the top governing bodies, that football learnt from these tragedies and that they never happened again.

In the 1993–94 season, some players left, others were injured, the young recruits were being trained. But in Europe we had a very good run in the second edition of the rebranded UEFA Champions League. There were superb victories against AEK Athens, Steaua Bucharest and Galatasaray. But in the semi-final against AC Milan, we suffered a crushing defeat. Even if Monaco had never got that far before, it's a painful memory which was added to by the bitterness of those dark years: the suspicions of corruption, fixed matches, the buying of referees and players, the open conflict between me and Olympique Marseille. The inquiry into the match-fixing scandal put a stop to the system that had lasted for years and poisoned everybody.

Even today I find it hard to talk about. How can I when there are such huge suspicions, when the certainties are not supported by any evidence, when those who know what happened and whom I urged to talk don't do so? How can one make a fair judgement about this so many years later, when French football and I have both come out of that dark time? I am thankful it hasn't dented my faith in the game, in sport, in humanity.

We knew at the time that it was a passing phenomenon that only concerned a small number of people. What mattered was standing firm and trying to trust your players when one might have been forgiven for suspecting them. And it was important that the suspicions did not change anything about the way we trained and played. And we couldn't be constantly suspecting our opponents, either. We knew Marseille was a great team with very good players, independent of what had or hadn't been done to help them win.

That unhealthy atmosphere, those squabbles between the players in the dressing room, those confidences shared about the involvement of this or that man, forced me to be fatalistic. We all needed to put aside our doubts and focus on those we could trust. I suppressed my anger. And I tried throughout that whole period never to suggest some presumed cheating as the explanation for a defeat, but on the contrary, to redouble our own efforts. I couldn't manage my players if I was suspicious. A coach is a guide, and in order to guide men you need to believe in them. I didn't want those terrible practices and years to affect my dream, to stain the beauty of the sport. Winning at any cost, that's something that would never occur to me to do, a practice I would never employ.

My departure from Monaco and my arrival in Japan did me a world of good. And I no longer feel the pain I felt at the time. That atmosphere of suspicion is dead and buried now, too. Those years are behind us, though. I'm sure they've left their mark and affected some people's opinion of the sport. When you have known so much injustice and frustration, you are in favour of anything that can assuage that doubt. I will always stand up for things to be fairer, even if it's at the expense of momentary excitement. That's not too high a price to pay. I've read a good deal of criticism of the video assistant referee (VAR), but I think it's a huge step forward. A lot of people claim that VAR kills the excitement and that in the past mistakes would just have balanced out over a season. That's an unacceptable argument, because there's no proof the mistakes do balance out, and even if that were the case, it would mean a mistake in itself isn't serious and even that we should accept large numbers of them.

On the contrary, to me, one way to forget and repair the damage done in those terrible years for French football is precisely to work hard for more justice and transparency.

Those years at Monaco were years of discovering victory, the excitement of European nights, and extreme rivalry. I stayed there for seven years, the longest tenure of any coach at Monaco. A few months earlier, I'd had to refuse an offer from Bayern Munich because I wanted to be fair to the club I loved, and to the players, and see out my contract. But the season had started out very badly, we'd had a lot more people injured, and by September 1994 the president had chosen to dispense with my services, knowing that in any case I wouldn't have gone any further after the end of my contract. I found that a bit unfair and brutal, but I knew it was part of the rigours of the profession.

The club has changed a lot today, because the context has changed, and therefore the directors' desire is to run the club as a business and no longer just put together a fine team. Today, profitability has to be achieved thanks to lucrative transfers, even if this means ransacking a team, destroying the work that has been accomplished. Everything changes, individuals come and go quickly: the owners, the coaches, the players – only the fans with their passion and their loyalty remain. New sports regulations along with this new ethos changed Monaco and the club that I coached. We're a long way from our 'style' and the Monégasque spirit of the early days.

As I left for Japan, I did however want to retain only those things that had been gained: the club over those years had changed its ambitions, established itself at the highest level, with wonderful players who had been trained and had started their careers there, and the last of these was not the least. Thierry Henry, whom I'd seen playing with the under-17s, had his major debut in 1994: he would go on to become that remarkable, sharp, intelligent player, with unbelievable physical strength, with whom I would soon be reunited at Arsenal. I also wanted to learn to transform what had been lost into lessons: the matches, the cups, sometimes a bit of innocence and optimism, which I was soon to rediscover at Nagoya.

'As in all Japanese culture, from flower arranging to sumo wrestling and baseball, my players were passionate about moves that were beautiful, precise and delicate. It was a quest for elegance and grace that I've always liked a lot.'

5

JAPAN

When I was the coach at Monaco, I lived in Villefranche-sur-Mer, overlooking the bay. It was idyllic. I had friends, and I had met Annie, the woman I would later marry and with whom in 1997 I would have a daughter, Léa. Annie Brosterhous often came to the stadium, and that was where we met. She was an athlete, a former basketball player. She had been married previously to a professional basketball player and they had two children together. When we met, she was a physical education teacher and she used to bring her classes to the stadium. Love developed gradually. We had both had a life before we met each other, we'd both been in relationships, both been single, and my freedom was the most important thing to me: I had learnt to live alone, I lived as I wanted according to my own rules, and I had a passion that took up all my time. But in Monaco, Annie and I got to know each other, we came to understand and find out about each other, to share our passion for sport, the discipline and the demands of the game. We saw more and more of one another, and when I later decided to go to Japan, she would come over and join me during the holidays.

In the autumn of 1994 I was doing some analysis of the recently completed World Cup for the FIFA technical committee. It was interesting work but not as all-consuming as the day-to-day involvement in club football. I had worked with players non-stop for years, and I was already missing coaching, the pitch, the matches. As beautiful as the Riviera was, neither the wonderful views nor the lifestyle could hold me captive and I felt ready to leave for a new club, far away. When people ask me if it was hard to go, to leave the bay of Villefranche, I tell this story that says it all about my personality, about the man that I was then. In Monaco, I had the most beautiful view but if I lost a match, I didn't see it. In Japan, I had a comfortable apartment but the window in my bedroom looked out on a wall, and that was it. I didn't see that either. Yet if I won a match, the wall would look like the most beautiful view in the world.

It was the agent Milan Ćalasan, a former Red Star Belgrade

and Dinamo Zagreb player, who put me in touch with the Grampus Eight club in Nagoya. I knew of the young J.League that had been formed in 1993 and was then flying high: it attracted incredible players, like Leonardo, who played for Kashima Antlers, and Dunga, who was at Júbilo Iwata. The J.League had a lot of money, paying players and coaches better than in Europe, which is no longer the case today. I indicated that I was prepared to travel out there, that I was curious to find out about the club but that I was not at all sure I would be able to accept the offer.

I set off with only Milan for company. I visited the city and the club. It was a rough industrial city, with no particular attractions. My immediate thought was that I hoped I would feel good at the club because Nagoya was certainly not a tourist destination! The club had turned professional in the same year the J.League was created. It was founded in 1939 as Toyota Motor SC. The club had a corporate mindset. When the players became pros, they were playing for the company. And they were prepared to die for the club and for the company. There was a very strong esprit de corps. But I was also aware – and I saw this at the home match that I attended – that the club was in major difficulty. They were known as the dead weight of the J.League. The team had lost seventeen matches in a row. There was no danger of relegation because there was no second division, but the club was bottom of the league. They lost the match I watched, too. I could sense their commitment, but they were disorganised and lacked good players: a holding midfielder, a creative midfielder, a quality centre-back, and ideally a reliable goalkeeper. I saw the team's potential, the good feeling in the club, the relationship of trust I could build with the directors and the huge amount of work required, all of which pleased me.

The following day, we had a meeting about the contract and the terms they were offering me. I headed back to Villefranche undecided, having asked for two or three weeks to think about it. I had taken videocassettes of their matches to analyse the team, work out as far as I could what was lacking and how I could best contribute to the club, given the freedom to do so. I was ready to give this adventure a go.

Right away, before leaving for Japan and starting my new job, I set to work looking for the players the club was lacking. I travelled to Brazil where I knew I'd be able to find one or two promising players within the budget that they had allocated me.

In São Paulo, I spent hours and hours watching matches and recordings of matches. One day, an agent brought me a tape and said to me: 'Take a look at this centre-back. He's the one for you.' I watched the match but it was the centre-back from the opposing team who immediately caught my eye. The agent managed to organise a meeting the next day with the young player and his representative, who agreed to come from Rio to meet me. In the meantime, I'd watched other videos of his matches and I was convinced. He understood the game well, he anticipated well, he was tall and had a good technique – everything we needed. I didn't watch him play a match: I made the decision based solely on his performances in the videos. That young player was Alexandre Torres.

The meeting was scheduled for the following day at 2 p.m. I was not told the agent's name, and when they arrived together, I felt a bit uneasy. I knew that face. I asked him his name: it was Carlos Alberto, the captain of the legendary 1970 team, the famous Brazilian right-back. He was Alexandre's agent and his father. Carlos was at loggerheads with the Brazilian Football Federation, which explained why his son didn't play for the national team. That reassured me about my choice! And when I subsequently saw him play, I was totally convinced. He was not only a very good player, he was also a man with an impeccable mentality and incredible class, who at the same time was very uncomplicated. He and his father became friends of mine and they often came to see me at Arsenal.

Before leaving Rio to join my partner Annie and my parents in Alsace for the Christmas holidays, I found out that Serbia were over to play a match against Brazil. I stayed to see if I might find a good player in the Serbian team as well, and I missed the Christmas celebrations! Although I did not find anyone on that occasion, I knew that Nagoya Grampus Eight already had an outstanding but under-utilised Serbian player by the name of Dragan Stojković. If I helped him progress as a player and he was willing to progress himself, he stood a good chance of recapturing his previous form.

Along with Alexandre Torres, I found two other players who were ready to come along with me for the adventure, two Frenchmen I knew well: Gérald Passi, an attacking midfielder, and Franck Durix, another midfielder. Passi had played with me at Monaco and I had seen Durix play at Cannes. I negotiated Franck's transfer with the city of Cannes and brought the director of Nagoya over for the signing in Nice. But just as we were about to sign, I sensed the Japanese director was hesitant. 'Perhaps the player is not so good,' he said to me. That was the moment I almost didn't go to Japan. It was the kind of moment everyone will have experienced, when even things that appear to be under control, and which have been patiently negotiated, can suddenly swing the other way. The eighteen months at Nagoya might never have happened. For me, it was a matter of principle. I gave the director ten minutes to think it over and sign the player's transfer or I would rescind my contract as coach. They brought in Durix and they had never regretted it.

Durix and Passi were two highly talented players. I knew exactly what they could bring to the team and to the Japanese game, and I knew exactly what the Japanese league could offer each of them. It was a new opportunity for everyone. After the dark years of French football, going to Japan was a way of escaping and, for foreign players, it was an opportunity to discover a league in its infancy, and a different game, and to have the freedom to express themselves. I know that this Japanese experience changed their lives as it changed mine.

A few weeks after I had settled in Nagoya with the players I had chosen, Boro Primorac arrived to be my assistant. I knew his enormous qualities as a player in Yugoslav club football and latterly in France at Lille and Cannes. I knew he was an upstanding and passionate man, but it was in Japan that I discovered his qualities as a coach, and it was there that our partnership, which would continue at Arsenal, was formed. We had the same vision of football. He was incredibly knowledgeable about team sports. At training sessions, he guessed what I wanted before I'd said a word. He also had a natural curiosity that meant he could live anywhere, adapt to any situation, and be accepted by the players, who liked him a lot. We had both come to Japan without our partners, who joined us during the holidays. We lived together when they were not there. We developed a system that ensured we were never alone; we lived for football and for work. Living together for those eighteen months sealed our friendship and our way of working. I remember one particular story that says a lot about the two of us and also about my father. My parents had come to Arsenal and we had organised a dinner with Boro and our respective families. Boro and my father were deep in conversation with each other for the entire evening. Later on, I asked my father what they had been talking about. He admitted that he had barely understood a thing Boro had said. It was as if Boro and I spoke a language that only we could understand. And that language was born in Japan!

Before the season began, I took all the foreign players and Japanese staff to a training camp on Okinawa Island. I wanted to keep only twenty players out of the thirty-five that were there with me. I knew that by reducing the squad, the team would be better organised, stronger. But I was faced with a terrible dilemma: during the training sessions, their physical effort, their attitudes would have justified my keeping them all. They were flawless. They had an unbelievable will to work, to progress. I knew I was going to be dropping men with a will of iron, a total grasp of the effort required and a devotion to their club that I've only ever seen in Japan. During the eighteen months I was there, I saw this absolute investment, this unremitting work in all the players. We had to hide the footballs to make sure the players didn't tire themselves out before the real training session began. This understanding of the effort that was required rubbed off on the foreign players as well. Dragan, for example, had not been used by the team for months at that point. I knew that if he wanted to return to form, he would have to work very hard. I made him suffer at the training sessions, but he threw himself completely into his preparation. He stuck with it and it paid off: he became a star in Japan in his seven-year career with Nagoya, so much so that some years later he would become the team's manager.

After those few days on the island and those weeks of preparation, we played our first friendly against São Paulo. At the time, Brazil were the world champions. So it was a test for us. I had started applying my methods, giving my instructions and, most of all, communicating my love for the game: I wanted to see where the team stood. Although we were vulnerable at the back, we beat them! The match confirmed what I felt, and reassured me: I had seen the players' potential. But when the league got under way, it was a catastrophe: we lost match after match. After eight weeks, we only had three points and languished at the foot of the fourteen-club league. The players had no confidence in themselves and I could see the moment coming when the directors would lose confidence in me. I was called into a meeting and I remember saying to Boro: 'I think we can pack our bags.' The directors and I agreed that the results had been very disappointing, I expected to hear that I was being fired . . . But instead they announced they were firing my interpreter! If I was unable to communicate my values and my instructions, it must be his fault! I fought for him to stay, the directors accepted my point of view, and we won that particular battle. I think the directors also gave me some time on the basis that the season couldn't be worse than the previous one. I had a bit of breathing space before we were likely to equal the current record of seventeen defeats in a row. The directors also saw just how involved I was in the club and in the J.League. I worked all the time and I wanted to help structure and develop the league.

I changed the central defence to counter our vulnerability at the back. When I put Go Oiwa with Alexandre Torres we were much more effective. And first and foremost, I tried to restore the players' lost confidence, to encourage them to rely on their strengths, their obvious talent, rather than always being scared of their opponents. The players were determined, tough and agile. They were very hard-working, with an iron discipline and huge respect for everything I was able to teach them. As in all Japanese culture, from flower arranging to sumo wrestling and baseball, my players were passionate about moves that were beautiful, precise and delicate. It was a quest for elegance and grace that I've always liked a lot. They were light on their feet. They just lacked power and sometimes favoured aesthetics over efficiency. But they could compensate for these flaws by being even more precise, agile, light and resilient. Their strong points needed to become even stronger. That's something I've tried to teach all my teams: cultivating their strengths and qualities, bringing them to the fore to compensate for any deficiencies, not doubting. The Nagoya team had another instinctive quality that I would see in England, too: a very strong team spirit, a natural desire to help others. And to win together.

I also learnt to compromise, to adapt my values and my coaching to their traditions, their beliefs. And I learnt to express my demands differently so that they would really hit home and be even more effective. Once again, it was an invaluable learning experience; at Monaco and other clubs, I had probably been a bit inflexible, hard, authoritarian. I adapted, I sought ways to compromise and understand, and this process of thinking about the game, about the best possible coaching methods, the particular culture of each country and even each club, enabled me to progress, to be more precise, to improve my coaching methods, to understand how better to communicate the messages that really needed communicating – how to train, how to prepare for a match, how what you know is the key to winning – and what I could adapt or change, the principles I could afford to drop.

So I had to make compromises. In Europe, for instance, football players, and athletes in general, are told not to have a hot bath the day before a match. But in Japan, saunas and ofuros, boiling-hot baths, are an age-old tradition. The first time the players stayed in the baths for hours, I was alarmed. But I said nothing: you have to learn to respect traditions.

I also had to be careful not to offend my players and my assistants. Honour is all-important to the Japanese. Not losing face was vital for them. If a coach tells his player that he played badly and was useless, the player loses face because he works on the principle that he always gives of his best. I had to find the appropriate language to express my dissatisfaction, my criticisms, without causing offence. And if I could not find the right words, I knew my interpreter would do it for me.

The other personality trait I had to adapt to was their huge discipline and commitment to hard work. These are positive qualities, of course, but if taken to extremes they can also become pitfalls. For instance, they had such respect for the coach that they expected everything of me. They applied my instructions to the letter but never dared take the initiative. They thought I was going to tell them what to do at every moment, and because I didn't, they were lost at first. I had to show them I was there to prepare them to take the best decisions, but that it was up to them to take those decisions. They had to develop the freedom to express themselves. And so we were able to develop a team style based on speed and mobility, relying on their technique and their intelligent creation and use of space.

I also told them they would only succeed if they trained and trained, but I never thought they would do so with such perseverance. I've never seen willpower like it. It was the only time I've ever had to develop strategies to hide footballs and ban players from playing before training sessions started, to stop them driving themselves so hard.

We all had to adapt, to make compromises, and that was when we started to win. The players adapted to my methods and values, and I also made concessions to them and their culture. It was an invaluable experience. I learnt to live a long way away from my friends and family, not in the more cosmopolitan Tokyo, but in a provincial Japanese city where I learnt to recognise the billboards and use them to navigate the forty-minute drive from my apartment to the stadium, praying that the adverts would not change, otherwise I would get lost! They did change, of course, but by then I'd learnt the journey off by heart. I also recall my first press conference in a traditional restaurant: no chairs, no benches, we sat on our heels on the floor. After ten minutes, I thought I was going to die. It felt much harder than any training session. I left the room every five minutes: they must have thought I was ill. I discovered their utter respect for timetables, their rigour, their discipline – never a late train, never an evening out that ran later than the time shown on the invitation. It was a culture shock but in a good way. I discovered extreme honesty, tact, a lifestyle that was like a dream after the previous difficult years at Monaco.

I also discovered an aspect of Japanese culture that was invaluable to me when it came to my relationship to football, to the game, and to success. Sumo wrestling is an age-old sport, with rituals and rules that have not changed since it was first invented. I often watched fights and I learnt a lot. Respect is a fundamental value of sumo wrestling. There are six tournaments a year. You have to win two to become a yokozuna. But the winning sumo wrestler then has to go before a judging committee that assesses whether his behaviour has been beyond reproach. Competitiveness is important but it is not enough on its own. A victorious sumo wrestler also has to behave impeccably. I have never forgotten that, and it seemed to me that this was crucial in football as well. I felt it freed me from the pressure of achieving a result at any cost and allowed me to rediscover the pure enthusiasm for the game, the enthusiasm I'd had as a child.

Another aspect of sumo wrestling and its rites is that a draw is impossible. Bouts had to end in victory or defeat. The J.League's rules have moved on now, but back then every match that ended in a draw was followed by extra time and a penalty shootout. This also gives some idea of the players' passion and investment in the game.

During those eighteen months in Japan, I cut myself off from my friends and family, from the pressure of Ligue 1, from the kind of brutality and violence to be found in European football. I didn't become a very different coach from the one who had pursued his passion at Monaco and at Nancy, but I lived for the game and the game only. I didn't read the press. I had no idea what was being said about me. I didn't suffer the intrusion of news stories about perceived slights or injustices. I could return to the essence of our profession. Being disconnected from the constant comments, advice, criticism and praise gave me a feeling of freedom. When I arrived at Arsenal, I thought I'd be able to avoid getting immediately caught up in the constant pressure, that I'd be less of a victim of all those who surround this passion. Of course, I fell back into it all immediately. But having experienced this kind of peace and serenity in Japan was a huge help to me during the very intense, very tough periods that were to come.

We rose rapidly from fourteenth to fourth, then second place! It was an extraordinary ascent. It united the team and gave everyone confidence. In the second half of the season, we sustained this successful performance, and kept up the good results. We won the Emperor's Cup in 1995, and then the Japanese Super Cup the following year. When I left in late September 1996, the team was well positioned to win the league championship: it was a close contest. We finished second. I remember there was such frenzy in the stadium, it was wonderful. We rediscovered the joy of the game, the purity of the game, playing in packed stadiums. These are very powerful memories: total fervour, silence and sometimes just a single tear rolling down the supporters' faces when we lost. The passion and enthusiasm of the fans and the players made every match feel like a European Cup night. There wasn't an empty seat in the stadium.

It was an amazing season, though clouded by an injury to a very good player, the striker Takafumi Ogura. He had torn the cruciate ligament in his knee while playing with the under-21 team during the mid-season break. I was in Nice at the time. He was operated on, and it went badly. He did come back, but never recaptured his previous form, power and style. He did not have the career he deserved. Ensuring that injured players could access the best treatment, and be operated on by the best surgeons so that top-flight players like Ogura were not lost to badly treated injuries, was a constant concern.

In June 1996, David Dein, Peter Hill-Wood and Danny Fiszman came out to Nagoya to meet me on behalf of Arsenal. I had already known David for some years. I had decided to return to Europe only on the condition that I went to a big club, and that it was a real challenge. Arsenal was a sizeable one. Within an hour we came to an agreement. I would join the London club as soon as possible, but I would not abandon Nagoya mid-season without a manager.

The Japanese directors hurried in a leisurely fashion to find a replacement for me! They didn't try to keep hold of me in the usual way. They deployed persuasive arguments: they had decided to make Japan the strongest footballing nation in . . . a hundred years' time. I was a cog, a part of their plan! That tells you all you need to know about how they relate to time, about their staying power and their determination. But as far as I was concerned, the decision was taken. Arsenal. A decision that would change my life. How could I have imagined I was about to embark on an adventure that would last twenty-two years?

'Arsenal had the reputation in the English league as "boring Arsenal", with a slow playing style where the only thing that mattered was the result: going for the goals, marking and defending the rest of the time. Although I have to say this reputation was exaggerated, I did want to change the playing style, to introduce a constructive game based on greater technical solidity.'

6

A LIFE AT ARSENAL, MY HOME

My attraction to England, my passion for English football, go way back. I arrived at Arsenal on 1 October 1996, and that day changed my life. Arsenal would become my passion and my obsession, and would devour all my energy. I lived in London and all I saw was the training centre and the stadium.

You have to go back many years to understand what a huge impact that encounter had on me, the importance of that particular club, the turn my life was going to take, as if I'd been preparing for years to live in London, to live only for this club, to give myself to it completely.

*

I was seven, eight, nine years old, growing up in my little village in Alsace, already thinking only of football. On the television at school, and later in the family bistro and at home, we used to watch the cup finals in the legendary Wembley Stadium. Television was still in black and white in those days but the ball stood out brightly against the grass pitch that looked so beautiful, perfectly mown and maintained, while we were still roughly cutting the grass on our pitch with our horses pulling the mower behind them. It is a dazzling memory: for me, it is the definitive image of football. I think that as a child I promised myself I would one day step on to that turf, a promise that of course I never voiced out loud, not even to myself. England and Wembley seemed to belong to another planet, another world. Imagine how I felt decades later, two years after arriving at Arsenal, when I led my team out from the dressing room on to the pitch at Wembley for the first time. Deep down, I couldn't believe it. All of a sudden, I was face to face with my dream and my idea of football: the intensity of the event, the fervour of the supporters, the perfection of the grass pitch, the delicious tension of the players, the white ball – everything embodied to perfection. I played eight FA Cup finals in this legendary stadium and at the equally magnificent Millennium Stadium, Cardiff, and won seven, and nine Charity and Community Shield matches, of which we won seven. Each occasion was a moment of intense emotion, of wonder, as if I were still the child

124

watching the black and white screen, deeply moved by what he saw.

My stay in Cambridge when I was 29 had been decisive, too. I would never have become the Arsenal manager without those three weeks alone in an English city. There was nothing obliging me to spend my holidays in this way but I absolutely wanted to speak English, I had a feeling it would be important and I certainly couldn't imagine going through life without speaking several languages. The decision to go to England changed my life. When I talked to a friend of mine, she said: 'Go to Cambridge, that's the best place to study.' I flew over and took a train to Cambridge, with no idea where I was going to stay or which language school I would attend. I arrived in Cambridge and went round knocking on doors to find a room to rent in someone's house. I was lucky: a lady invited me in and suggested a school where I could enrol and sit some tests the following day. They put me in an intermediate group, and I was surrounded by teenagers, but the key thing was that my teacher was my landlady! She was my fairy godmother throughout my stay. I worked hard those three weeks. I wanted to be comfortable with the language, to attain the best possible level. I wanted my teacher/landlady to be proud of her student.

By the time I returned to Strasbourg, I had put so much effort into my English that I didn't want to lose it: I read books in English and I noted down all the words I didn't know so I could look them up in my dictionary. I did that for years. I read novels as well as lots of books on research, science and management. It proved very useful. Today, my daughter Léa, who grew up in England and attended state school until she was eleven, then the French Lycée, is doing research at Cambridge University, finishing her doctorate in neurosciences. I often go and visit her.

I have tried to find the house of the landlady who was so welcoming to me on that first visit and who gave me my first real English lessons, but my memory is fuzzy and I haven't been able to find it yet. She changed my life too.

It was David Dein who brought me to Arsenal. His father was a tailor and David himself had made his fortune in the sugar and coffee trade. When I met him in 1989, he was his beloved club's vice-chairman and main shareholder. He had been vice-chairman of the Football Association, and was one of the five people who created the Premier League. A few days before we first met, I had been in Turkey during the Christmas break from the football season in France to watch a Galatasaray match, as Monaco were scheduled to play them shortly after. The match took place in Konya on 31 December, and I spent that night in Ankara. Instead of returning to Nice, I decided to go to England and see a match during their busy Christmas schedule. I called Glenn Hoddle's agent and asked him to find me an interesting game. On New Year's Day I flew to London. That's how I ended up seeing my first match at Highbury: Arsenal–Norwich. Arsenal won, but the goals were not what I remember most about that evening. At the time, Arsenal was a very traditional club. In fact, the wives and guests were kept apart in a different room from the directors. I smoked back then. At half-time, I was chatting to a friend of David Dein's wife and she offered me a light.

And so, thanks to that cigarette, to my reasonable English that I'd learnt in Cambridge, and to that conversation, I found myself invited to David Dein's house that evening. He had said to me: 'We'll talk about football.' I mainly recall a very sociable evening with a lot of laughter and games, a kind of charades. I seem to recall one of the subjects they asked me to enact was *A Midsummer Night's Dream* – no easy task – and I got through it pretty well! The friendship, complicity and understanding between David and me date from that first dinner, and from all the times we've seen each other since.

David had a boat moored in Antibes that was called *Take It Easy* (he often joked he should have called it *Take It Please* because of all the money it cost him), and every time he came to the Côte d'Azur, we had some great times together. He would come to the Louis II Stadium to watch matches. He was curious about everything, and as passionate about football as I was. He realised that at Monaco we played a very different type of football from the football he saw at

Arsenal, and that intrigued him. He wondered whether that style of play could be exported to England. We could talk for hours about the game, about a match, about developments in the sport and our profession. At the time, English football didn't make any money from television, and the good players ended up abroad, as had happened with Glenn Hoddle at Monaco. English football was a direct, unembellished, fully committed style of football, a domestic game with teams consisting mostly of English players with a sprinkling from around the British Isles. It was a football with its own codes and rituals. The clubs belonged to wealthy English figures, families who passed them down from father to son and who respected the traditions of a game where elegance and fair play were very much present. Thanks to David Dein and Arsenal, I discovered these rituals and codes of behaviour, the frenzied fans, with not a single foreign manager, and clubs and players that as yet had little money.

By early 1995 I had left Monaco after seven years at the helm. Arsenal had parted company with their manager, George Graham – who had done so much to shape the club and build the team – fired for reasons unknown to me. David Dein invited me to meet Peter Hill-Wood, who had been the Gunners' chairman since 1982, following on from his father Denis and his grandfather Samuel. We all had dinner together before I left for Nagoya. I think they were sounding me out but were not yet ready to take on a foreigner. It was Bruce Rioch who took over from Graham. But it worked out badly, the club struggled a bit mid-table, and as I have mentioned it was in June 1996 that Peter Hill-Wood, David Dein and Danny Fiszman, a director of the club and one of the biggest shareholders, came to see me in Japan. This time they firmly expressed their desire to hire me and in an hour we had agreed on everything. That hour would shape my destiny.

Was I aware of the huge challenge this would be for me? Was I aware that this club would give me everything, and that I too would give it my time, all my energy, all my passion for twenty-two years – that, in short, Arsenal would be my home? Was I aware that all the years I'd spent coaching Nagoya from Strasbourg to Nagoya had in a way prepared me for this challenge, and that at Arsenal, to a greater and better extent than anywhere else, I was going to be able to apply my vision of management and, most of all, continue to develop the club?

A new season had already begun at Arsenal but I was still in Japan, honouring my commitment not to leave Nagoya without a manager. In my absence, my future assistant, Pat Rice, a former Arsenal player, was coaching them. I tried to do the player recruitment from Japan. That is how I brought in Rémi Garde and Patrick Vieira. They were not officially first-team players but they started the season without me. I called them, Pat and David every week, and was sent videocassettes of all the matches. With the time difference, it felt like I was permanently working, which was good preparation for when I would subsequently find myself working night and day at Arsenal.

Even from distant Japan I was already concentrating on what I was going to do in England. I was becoming aware of everything I would have to do to prove and assert myself, and show everyone what I was capable of. The directors were prepared to let me transform the club. They knew I had different ideas and they were well placed to know that the arrival of a total stranger, a foreigner, direct from Japan, was going to cause a stir, that it would be met with scepticism and generate a lot of opposition. In a way, they were braver than I was. I knew the welcome would be frosty, but that was how it was everywhere for any new manager and it was part of his job to gradually gain acceptance through his results and his values. I would fight the scepticism with the power of my convictions, my ideas, my capacity to adapt to the team and to get the best out of them. But the hostility was greater than I ever could have imagined and the directors had to deal with this, as did I.

When I left Japan for Arsenal, I changed continents, worlds, club and culture. What awaited me was life in a hotel, players who were wonderful but sceptical, vile rumours, and a minefield to be crossed. Today I know it was all worth it, and that my strength lay in my passion and in the kind of blissful unawareness that enabled me to concentrate on the next match, the players and my involvement in what I was already thinking of as my club.

From the videos I had watched in Japan, and as soon as I started training with them at the club, I had respect for the players. They were a group of highly experienced men, who had been trained for the most part by George Graham. They were intelligent, hard-working, and prepared to offer total commitment. It was a generation that had not earned a lot of money, whose whole careers were spent at one club and who, once they had signed their contract, gave their all to their team. They were the sons of humble, tough, proud families who had great respect for the club's culture and traditions. They were very closely knit, and they socialised together – not always keeping to the 'invisible training' rules, but I could clearly see they were very united. David Seaman, Tony Adams, Ray Parlour, Paul Merson, Martin Keown, Nigel Winterburn, Steve Bould, Lee Dixon . . .

I also discovered the club's very strong identity and distinctive history that had been passed down from generation to generation.

In 1886, the first team at the club consisted of factory workers from the Royal Arsenal in Woolwich, south-east London. In 1910, the club was bought by the businessmen Henry Norris and William Hall, and in 1913 it moved to the legendary ground at Highbury, north London, which was steeped in this history and the spirit of those who had left their mark on it, in particular Herbert Chapman, the manager who gave Arsenal their first league title in 1931. When I came to Arsenal, I discovered this man's story, his innovative techniques, his invention of the WM formation when the law of offside was changed, the way that he used physiotherapy, his ideas on training methods, numbered shirts and more modern studs, floodlighting, the list goes on. He even managed to have an Underground station, Gillespie Road, named after Arsenal. I liked his commitment. Everyone who worked at the club knew his life story, ending in his sudden death from pneumonia in 1934. His legacy was that Arsenal became the dominant English team of the decade.

I gradually came to understand the Arsenal identity and who its followers were: it was a club with a huge sense of tradition, where behaving with class was important, but which was also open to innovation. Arsenal was firmly embedded in the local community and had very solid, working-class foundations. The fans espoused the club's values. This visceral attachment, from childhood, to a club and a team is something I have never seen anywhere else with such fervour. Every supporter's first match at Highbury was like a baptism. Supporters had two kinds of tattoos: the name of their club and the names of their children. I also remember the story of the heroic fan who put his own life in danger to stop a man on the Tube from killing himself.

Immediately after saving the man, he jumped on the next train, because the match had already started and he didn't want to miss it. For me, that says everything about the Arsenal spirit.

The first Arsenal match I attended after agreeing to manage the club was at the Müngersdorfer Stadium, Cologne, on 25 September 1996. Arsenal were playing Borussia Mönchengladbach. I was there as an observer, as I wasn't yet officially in post. I was with David Dein, and we were watching from the stands. At half-time, the teams were level and I went down to the dressing room. Pat Rice asked me to speak to the players and I decided to change the defence and bring off Tony Adams, the team captain. This surprised and perhaps destabilised them, and we lost the match. I might have hoped for better for my first contact, but I did get fired up by what was at stake and the challenge we had to face together.

Arsenal had the reputation in the English league as 'boring Arsenal', with a slow playing style where the only thing that mattered was a result: going for the goals, marking and defending the rest of the time. Although I have to say this reputation was exaggerated, I did want to change the playing style, to introduce a constructive game based on greater technical solidity.

When I arrived, Arsenal lay in mid-table. The teams that dominated the league were Manchester United, Newcastle

United and Liverpool. I had watched many videos of the team's matches when I was in Japan and I could also base my ideas on the match I had seen in person. I was able to assess the quality of the team and see how to organise them, how to raise their level. I had also understood how united the team was, and I did not want them to unite against me.

A few weeks later, on 12 October 1996, I was no longer in the stands – it was my first real match as manager: we were playing away at Blackburn Rovers. Ian Wright scored twice. Victory! On the way to the stadium, the players were chanting: 'We want our Mars bars!' I had started to work with them and apply my ideas, particularly as regards nutrition. For the players, it was a real change, both in coaching methods but also in the more regular sessions, the meals we ate together, the nutrition lessons and the muscle-strengthening exercises.

I knew I had to progress in small steps, gradually taking the team in hand, applying diplomacy and psychology, without relinquishing my convictions. I also knew there were people waiting for a chance to trip me up and that, like the press asking 'Arsène who?', they were entirely within their rights to question what I would be able to bring them, whether I was any good. That first victory was crucial in my eyes. It allowed me to establish my vision from the outset, and to reinforce my legitimacy as a coach.

*

It was a team of thirty-somethings, all tough men, but the training needed to be adapted because they had already given a great deal. They were competitors and winners. We did x-rays of their knees and ankles, and there were some people who said these players should have stopped playing a long time ago. But they were passionate about continuing, and in the training we needed to make the most of their love for competition to get them to progress. Their convictions and feelings came out in their playing style, and they fought hard to overcome their deficiencies. They liked the competition more than the training. I tried to make the training sessions appealing and show them that if they threw themselves into it, it could prolong their playing careers. For this to happen, they needed to be persuaded to give up their bad habits. The timing was right for my ideas. There was a big drinking culture in the club, but England in the 1990s and 2000s was ready for change. Society had embarked on a health drive, and within the club, everyone was aware of the need for major changes.

Tony Adams was a legendary Arsenal captain. He was coming off alcohol and required attention. He had authority over the team and even over his opponents. He had an incredible understanding of the defensive game; he was always ahead, intelligent, a fighter, with a combination of confidence and huge doubt. He was surrounded by fantastic defenders like Lee Dixon, Nigel Winterburn, Steve Bould and Martin Keown. Tony was battered and physically damaged, and he didn't like training. I never knew whether he was going to be able to play on the Saturday, like an actor who doesn't rehearse his part, but on matchday he was always there. I regularly sent him out to the physiotherapist Tiburce Darou in the south of France for intensive treatment and physical preparation sessions.

Then there was David Seaman, David the Atlas, classy, loved by those who worked with him, the legendary goalkeeper, and his mentor Bob Wilson. David had a heavy build but perfect physical mastery.

Dennis Bergkamp, the club's unconditional idol, a perfectionist whom I never saw make a careless technical move, had arrived a year before me, bought from Inter Milan. He had had a difficult first season but I knew he was a fantastic player, that he needed to be given the ball and that he needed to control the game to show all he was capable of. Dennis, a great player, saw things fast, moved fast, decided fast and executed with perfection and elegance.

There was Ian Wright, the incredible striker those around him sometimes found hard to control, his opponents especially. He was an extrovert, hyperactive, and had endured an extremely hard life. His playing style was instinctive, and he had the killer instinct, a player like no other.

Then there was Martin Keown, a man who harboured a huge desire to push himself, to progress. He was constantly dissatisfied with his performance, and always trying to learn how to be better. He listened to others, because he knew

With members of the Coupe de France-winning team. Standing
with me from left to right are Ramón Díaz, Roger Mendy, Emmanuel
Petit, Claude Puel, Franck Sauzée and Jean-Luc Ettori; seated from
left to right are Gérald Passi, Youri Djorkaeff, George Weah,
Luc Sonor and Rui Barros.

With Prince Rainier and Prince Albert of Monaco during
a dinner to celebrate winning the trophy.

REGLES DE DIETETIQUE

Important : 1) - Eviter de boire en mangeant - un verre de vin à la
fin des principaux repas suffit - boire entre les
repas et au moins une 1/2 h avant de manger.

2) - Eviter l'absorption en même temps de légumes verts
et de pommes de terre.

3) - Eviter le café au lait ou le thé au lait : indigeste

RATION-TYPE EN PERIODE D'ENTRAINEMENT

Petit déjeuner
(entre 7 h et 8 h)
(café noir au réveil)
- Céréales au lait sucré
- Pain grillé - confiture - beurre
- Jus de fr uit ou Fruit

Déjeuner
entre 12 h et 13 h.
- Crudité ou légume cuit assaisonné (citron-huile)
- Viande ou Poisson ou Foie
- 1 féculent ou 1 légume vert
- 1 fromage
- 1 fruit ou compote

Goûter
17 h
- Thé ou café léger ou lait
- Biscottes ou Biscuits secs

Diner
19 à 20 h
- Potage aux légumes passés
- Viande ou Poisson ou 2 oeufs au jambon
- 1 légume vert ou 1 féculent (suivant le menu de midi)
- 1 salade ou 1 fruit
- 1 entremets au lait ou 1 yaourt

Quantités à prendre chaque jour

Pain : 300 gr - P.d.t. : 400 gr
Céréales : 30 gr - Sucre : 50 gr - Confiture : 50 gr
Viande : 250 à 300 gr - Lait : 0 l 400
Fromage : 60 gr - Beurre : 30 gr - Oeuf : 1/2
Légume vert : 500 gr - Fruit : 150 gr
Agrumes : 150 gr

Au moins : 1 repas par semaine prendre du foie
- à la place de la viande
2 à 3 repas par semaine prendre du poisson.

A diet sheet for before and after a match, from my time at Monaco.

LA VEILLE DU MATCH

- repas habituels mais remplacer de préférence la viande par du foie de veau et éviter les féculents ainsi que les boissons alcoolisées.

APRES LE MATCH

- **Boire** : 300 gr d'eau de Vichy contenant 1 gr de sel
- **Eviter** : toute boisson alcoolisée ou riche en gaz carbonique
- **Prendre** : 1/2 heure avant le diner 1/2 1 d'eau d'Evian

- **Au dîner** :
  - 1 bouillon de légumes salé
  - 1 plat de pâtes ou de riz ou de P.d.t. avec 15 gr de beurre frais
  - 1 salade verte à l'huile ou au citron avec 1 oeuf dur
  - 1 ou 2 tranches de pain (hypazoté) ou biscottes
  - 1 ou 2 fruits mûrs
  - 1 verre de bordeaux

LE LENDEMAIN

- **Petit déjeuner** : - 1 gr. tasse de café léger ou thé sucré avec
  (10 h)   biscottes
  - 1/4 1. de jus de fruit frais

- **Déjeuner** : - 1 légume crû - 1 plat de pâtes ou riz servi avec beurre ou fromage râpé
  - 1 salade à l'huile ou au citron - Fruits mûrs ou secs
  - 1 verre de vin
- **A 16 h** : - 1/4 1 de jus de fruit
- **Diner** : - Habituel avec viande ou poisson

LE SURLENDEMAIN

- Les 4 repas doivent être copieux - Petit déjeuner habituel, plus 1 tranche de jambon - Déjeuner habituel, plus gâteu de riz ou de semoule - Diner habituel, plus fromage.

- Les autres jours, retour au régime normal.

Dining in Japan with my longtime assistant Boro Primorac and our translator Go Murakami.

With the Nagoya Grampus team after the Emperor's Cup in 1996. From left to right in the front row are Franck Durix, Yusuke Sato, Drajan Stojkovic, Tetsuya Asano, Tetsuya Okayama and Takashi Hirano; and with me behind them are Boro Primorac, Takafumi Ogura, Yasuyuki Moriyama and Alexandre Torres.

Above With my
daughter Léa.

Right With
Annie and Léa.

Left 'What does this Frenchman know about football? He wears glasses and looks more like a schoolteacher?' – Tony Adams

Below With captain Tony Adams in 1998 when we achieved the Double of Premier League champions and FA Cup winners.

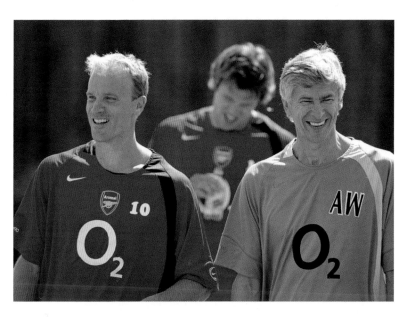

With Dennis Bergkamp

Signing Thierry Henry from Juventus in August 1999.

'An example to follow.' I didn't want an unfair Cup result against Sheffield United to stand, so the club offered to replay the tie. (*L'Équipe*, 24 February 1999)

that would enable him to progress. He was often caught up in an intense rivalry with Tony Adams, who was born the same year – 1966 – but it was a positive rivalry.

In addition to these players already at the club, whose intelligence and intrinsic qualities were obvious to me, I wanted, while I was still in Japan, to bring in new players, new recruits capable of integrating into this group and coping with the intensity of the Premier League. Having initially brought in Patrick Vieira and Rémi Garde, they were followed by Emmanuel Petit and Gilles Grimandi the following year.

We bought Patrick Vieira from AC Milan just as he was about to sign for Ajax in Amsterdam. I managed to convince him and his agents Marc Roger and Jean-François Larios that he should come to Arsenal. He had made a huge impression on me as a young player in Cannes when I was the Monaco coach. He had found it difficult to break into the first team and Milan let him go. And he trusted us. Right from his very first match, when he was as yet unknown to the English public, he showed just how talented he was. No one disputed his ability, and he gave me the credibility and the hold over the club that I needed in order to take it in the direction I wanted. He and Emmanuel Petit became a duo that would remain forever etched in the memories of Arsenal supporters. And in a sense, they came into their own at Arsenal and the club changed their lives too, because they were selected for the French national team in the same configuration, and displayed their immense talent to the world. Petit was the great player of the 1998 World Cup.

Emmanuel Petit and Tony Adams got on very well together. They had a similar sensitivity and liking for competition, an incredible mastery. They knew how to go above and beyond.

I already knew Rémi Garde. He had played at Lyon and Strasbourg and I thought he was excellent. He was often injured and unfortunately he did also suffer injury at Arsenal, but he was fast, he was good in duels and he too was an excellent influence on the team.

Throughout this adventure, players would join the club and leave their mark on its history. Notable among them, were:

- Freddie Ljungberg, a man capable of punching holes in the opposition defence, an incredible winner. I bought him from Halmstad after seeing him on television playing for Sweden against England one weekend. He was up against Martin Keown in that match and had occasionally put him in difficulty. Martin was very good in one-to-ones, which showed the worth of Freddie. I watched the match twice and immediately decided to buy him on the Monday after the match. It was one of my great moments of madness!

- Gilberto Silva, calm strength, serving the team with class and humility.
- Andrey Arshavin, a creative dribbler, a Russian genius, bought on transfer deadline day early in February 2009. The four goals he scored against Liverpool at Anfield in April that year will remain forever etched in the memories of the supporters who witnessed it.
- Aaron Ramsey, who arrived from Cardiff at the age of seventeen; his career stalled when he was nineteen after a broken leg in a match at Stoke, but he nonetheless went on to have a great career at Arsenal, thanks to his energy and creativity, scoring two FA Cup final-winning goals.
- William Gallas, uncompromising defender and goalscorer at decisive moments.
- Bacary Sagna, a full-back with incredible courage who would become a key player.
- Thomas Vermaelen, centre-back brought in from Ajax, later transferred to Barcelona, team captain with irreproachable behaviour.
- Theo Walcott, explosive, with good sense and intelligence when calling for the ball, whose development would unfortunately be impacted by numerous injuries.
- Per Mertesacker, life and soul of the team and the dressing room, who would never stop progressing as a centre-back.

- Łukasz Fabiański, super-talented goalkeeper whose sensitivity was sometimes a handicap.

- Gaël Clichy, recruited from AS Cannes, a left-back whose faultless attitude enabled him to progress constantly.

- Kieran Gibbs, wholly trained at the club, another very gifted left-back, fast and with great technique, but also really lacking in confidence.

- Francis Coquelin, a defensive midfielder with good ball-recovery skills, who would improve a great deal technically throughout his career.

- Wojciech Szczęsny, who trained at the club as a young goalkeeper, a big talent who has now reached maturity at Juventus.

- Pascal Cygan, from Lille, left-sided centre-back, who had a good career at the club.

- Philippe Senderos, Swiss centre-back with an exemplary attitude who was part of the 2006 Champions League epic.

- Nwankwo Kanu, Nigerian genius, creative, technical, brave, a player everyone admired.

From the moment I started working at Arsenal, all I thought of was what we could improve. I shut myself away from the world and devoted my life to the club, and that took up all my time. It was the start of twenty-two years of passion and determination.

Since my early years in Alsace, my own training had

been a succession of lessons and apprenticeships. Coping with defeats as best I could, winning a match, selecting and training players, selecting and training a team, giving a team its own style, winning a title, leaving a club . . . I had done all that as I went along.

Behind this passion and immense pleasure, constant effort was required, and it was accompanied by moments of pain and loneliness that were sometimes difficult to take. But all art contains an element of pain and requires a taste for effort. Today, huge emphasis is placed on winning and losing, and throwaway comments take on exaggerated importance. People tend to disregard the massive amount of work required for each match. I was prepared to pay a heavy price for Arsenal, and time has shown I did just that. It was my choice to put myself totally at the service of football. When I arrived in England at the age of 47, I already had a certain maturity and confidence when it came to dealing with difficulties. I felt I was more measured, more level-headed than before. I knew I would have difficult decisions to make, huge challenges, ordeals to face, but I was even stronger and more robust than I had been at Monaco or in Japan. I was ready to face anything.

Of course I understood the reservations people might have had about my appointment to the top spot in the club. The 'Arsène who?' headlines in the papers and the questions on the lips of the players and the supporters felt legitimate. I could respond to this with hard work, commitment and my convictions. But when it came to the pure hostility, lies, vile allegations, defamation and harassment, there was nothing I could do but let the storm blow over.

It all started with a radio presenter, a Spurs supporter, so I have been told. I had apparently been spotted in disreputable locations, in preposterous situations, and the newspapers had incriminating photos. Flabbergasted, I asked them to produce the photos.

I was still living alone in the hotel. My partner Annie had remained in the south of France. In the breakfast room at the hotel, people avoided me, and many suspicious looks were directed my way. As always in cases like these, there were some objective journalists, and there were others who do not deserve a mention. Some went so far as to question my family, former team members, players and clubs where I had been in the past; they even went to Annie's house in Roquebrune-Cap-Martin in the south of France and waited for her to go out to question her son who was twelve years old at the time and ask him how I behaved around him, what kind of stepfather I was. It was intolerable. I wondered whether the world had gone mad, how such lies could be written without any evidence or truth, just to smear a man with no regard for the possible consequences. I was very angry. But this is sometimes the fate of people in the public eye.

Those journalists did not stop there: taking advantage

of one of my trips to Alsace, they then published the information that I had resigned and had gone home. When I returned to London, the taxi driver who drove me to the club seemed surprised I was back. At the club, I was greeted by the PR manager, who appeared ill-at-ease: 'Why didn't you tell me about your resignation?' I was staggered. I held an impromptu press conference on the steps of Highbury. I told them I was not afraid, that I was ready to confront and refute lie after lie, that the only things that mattered to me were the interests of the club.

Time went by, and further lies were published. After one match, I was forced to raise my voice to make myself heard above a barrage of questions. I reiterated my faith in football and my conviction that England was something other than a country capable of approving of a lynching of this kind, that for me the English were honest and respectful people, and that I had nothing to hide. And suddenly everything stopped, as unexpectedly and abruptly as it had started.

I'll say it again: inside the club and with my players I felt at home. I had the total trust of David Dein, and the players did not utter a word about my personal business. But outside the club, I could not have imagined a tougher welcome. I ignored the slander, the insults. Afterwards, this dreadful period would serve as a lesson to me, strengthening my determination and my energy at work. I had stood my ground despite the brutality of the moment. I saw to it that this ordeal did not destabilise me, the players or the club, nor did it affect my optimism, my values. And I tried to understand: could such an outburst of violence be explained by the fact that I was a foreigner, an unknown, that I had this coveted job and that people were jealous? Does the world of football carry such violence within it? Does the blame lie with those who do not belong to this world and who just comment on it? I don't have the answer.

I was alone throughout all those very long weeks. Boro had not yet arrived from Japan, Annie was not yet living with me, and my family and friends were in France, unaware of what I was going through. I had only myself to rely on, and that was a lesson, too.

Once the libellous things written by the journalists had stopped, I rediscovered a kind of serenity but I stayed on my guard. This was another precious lesson I tried to convey to others: in our profession you should always be wary. When you speak to players, journalists, fans, you should be careful with your words and gestures, and that was how I approached press conferences. I knew what to expect because I had come through the worst. The art of the press conference is to respond while remaining prudent. Primarily, you have to be vigilant about protecting the club and group unity. Managers deal with the press a lot, increasingly so in the world of football (when I left Arsenal there were six or seven press conferences a week, not to mention the interviews and club TV), and the press recognised a particular quality in me: I responded honestly, with as much authenticity as possible, and never hid away.

When we speak to the press, we are also speaking to our players, our supporters, our directors.

This episode also enabled me to protect my players from media attacks and difficult situations. Certain players sometimes hit the headlines with stories about drinking or women. I know you have to deal with these matters with dignity, always remain fair in your reactions, and think only of the objectives to be achieved. Your own emotional reactions must take a back seat, and if you bear a grudge, you lose lucidity and energy.

But the club stood firm and so did I.

We were facing some major challenges: transforming the team, getting the old and new players to work as a unit, raising the level, improving technical capabilities, and transforming the club. I was supported by David Dein, with whom there was clearly a close bond, and by Pat Rice, my assistant. Pat was devoted to his club and knew it inside out. We attended the morning and afternoon training sessions together, and in the first weeks he accompanied me to the office, an hour's drive away. My life in London was organised around the training centre, the office and the hotel, and later my small, comfortable house, with a typical English garden, a discreet house where I felt extremely good. These were the three pillars of my life in London and for years I knew nothing of the city. It was as if I lived in Arsenal and not in London.

That first year, the club's big challenge was to find another training ground. The grounds where we were training belonged to University College London! The club didn't own them, and we had to ask permission for everything. I felt our facilities were twenty years out of date, and did not reflect the great club we wanted to be. Every Sunday for a year, David and I looked for a place where we could build the new training centre, and in the end it was Ken Friar, the long-standing director of the club, who found the land. I was on site every day until it opened in 1999. We built ten pitches, and a modern, functional, harmonious building, because we wanted to offer the team the best. Everything down to the smallest detail was therefore important to me.

Alongside Pat Rice, I had Boro to count on once he came over from Japan to join me as deputy at Arsenal. He knew the way I worked. He got on with everyone. He is a modest man, with an outstanding knowledge of the game and the players, and he was someone who worked for the good of the group. He was a man I could rely on, and he offered me unwavering support. He was always there during difficult moments, and there were plenty of those. We did not live together, as we had done in Japan. He and his wife had a house but I was always welcome there as he was at mine. He came over every week to watch matches, and when I left Arsenal and I was feeling alone and sad, I went round to their house for lunch nearly every day. A lifelong friendship.

Boro, Pat Rice and I put in place a team with a desire to win, with ambitions, rigour and a playing style that we wanted everyone to be clear about. Around the team there were external specialists I considered the best in their fields. That enabled me to maintain a lightweight structure. I brought in a doctor, Yann Rougier, a specialist from the Paris hospital trust who was passionate about the neurosciences, nutrition, and psychoneuroimmunology. He was a founding member of IN2A, the Institute of Applied Neuronutrition and Neurosciences. I had known him since my Monaco days. I was very interested in anything that could improve performance, beyond standard training. I felt we had quite good mastery of everything that happened on the pitch but much less off it, and there was plenty of room for improvement. The two of us had very different temperaments but we were both passionate about science and experimentation, and we had worked together effectively for many years. He explained to the players how to eat, what to eat, how to chew. I had brought him over to Japan as well. Yann was one of the pioneers in the field of nutrition and the best at talking to the players. He had started to create menus at the club. There was a joke doing the rounds: I supposedly made the players eat broccoli morning, noon and night. It was not true, especially as I'm not all that keen on broccoli. However, it is true that Yann helped to drastically change the players' eating habits. For example, instead of the famous chocolate bars and fizzy drinks at half-time, we gave them caffeine drops on a sugar lump. Of course, they were hungry at first but they soon got over that. That had primarily enabled the players to improve the consistency of their performance and made them conscious of good dietary habits. Yann was later replaced by Hervé Castel, who was also extremely competent.

I also brought over an osteopath from Paris, Philippe Boixel, who worked with the French national team, top-flight clubs and the best players. He had trained as a physio and an osteopath. He helped players to recover more easily, to have a better approach to matches, and better stress management. He would spend two days a week at Arsenal, and examine all the players, the injuries and dislocated joints caused by knocks received during the matches.

Then there was an English psychologist, David Elliott, who came to the club every week, as well as Tim O'Brien, David Priestly and Dr Ceri Evans, who were also involved in working with the club to solidify the mental aptitudes of the team and the players.

This lightweight structure enabled the technical side of the club to be efficient, kept to a manageable size, and created a favourable environment for performance and progress. I've always been careful to surround myself with the best people in their particular fields, and to be able to rely on objective performance analysis tools. At Monaco, I was one of the first to promote Jean-Marc Guillou's analysis tool to guide a player's development, helping him more easily to identify those areas that required improvement. At Arsenal, we were also the first to sign up with ProZone, the first company to provide physical performance analysis. Today, that has become standard practice.

Everything we put in place needed to enable the team to raise its game, lift themselves up from the middle of the table and win the title.

After Patrick Vieira, Rémi Garde and Emmanuel Petit, another player was decisive in leading the team to the 1998 championship title: Nicolas Anelka.

The first time I met Anelka was at the PSG training centre. I had gone to France to buy a young player from Auxerre. My agents in France were talking to me about a promising young player who was not happy in Paris, who was not being played a lot. I met up with him. He was a shy 17-year-old, but he seemed determined to leave and he told me he wanted to come to Arsenal. I returned to England and waited; I had the feeling he might change his mind and want to stay at PSG. But two months later, he was still totally determined. I came to an agreement with PSG and we bought him. He arrived in February 1997. We had to get him to work, finish his training, toughen up, and integrate into the group. It was hard at first, but he made rapid progress.

The last match of the season, on 11 May, we were play-ing away at Derby County. I planned the team with him in mind. As I boarded the bus that was taking us to Derby, I saw that he was not there. I found him in his room, packing his bags. He was not happy, he felt he wasn't playing enough, he wanted to go home. We had a long conversation that was to change everything. I asked him not to give up yet. I told him he needed to carve out a place for himself with his playing skills, not with sudden bursts of brilliance, and not to run away at the first sign of difficulty. And I convinced him to stay.

The next day, Paul Merson was injured ten minutes into the match. I brought Anelka on, and he became one of the men of the match. In the dressing room after our victory, I found him with a huge celebratory smile on his face. I told him never to forget what had just happened in only twenty-four hours. The previous day, he had been thinking of dropping everything, today he was being feted as one of the powerhouses of the team.

After that, Nicolas became a star. But that story stayed with me. At moments when certain players were massively discouraged, I knew how quickly everything could change. And I must say, this has been confirmed frequently in my career.

A few weeks before that last match of the season, my life changed: I became a father. At the time, I was probably too busy with my work to realise that this was a blessing, but that's what Léa's birth definitely was.

Léa was born on 7 April 1997, in Monaco. In a way, she waited for me: we had a match against Chelsea that we won 3-0 on 5 April, after which I flew out to Monaco to be with Annie for the birth. Annie and Léa joined me in London at the end of the year and, all of a sudden, from the single life that I had been leading, we were building a family life for our daughter, a life we tried to protect to the best of our ability. Annie was amazing when it came to coping with a man like me who was so busy, so passionate about his job and inevitably a bit selfish: she gave Léa all her love, passed on all her values, she was an amazing mother. We have a friendly relationship and respect one another. I know exactly what I owe her, I know what she had to deal with, and I know that living with a man who was mad about his profession, who made football his religion, was not easy. I did not want to go through life without being a father, I wanted to have a child. But I have a number of regrets, as many fathers do: not having been present enough sometimes for Léa, and not having had more children. Léa has a brother, Kegan, and a sister, Erika. I like big families, I have memories of family reunions with lots of people, lots of laughter as well as arguments, and I know that families are a huge support in life because when you've got that, you never feel really alone.

Léa is a brilliant young woman, who has an innate

fondness for competition. She was so good at school that I hope she never finds my school reports. When she was small, any game I played with her always turned into a competition, and she put all her energy into beating me. She puts everything into her studies and into her athletics, for which she trains assiduously.

I have to say, Léa was a child with a lot of ability who worked impressively hard. She had a comfortable childhood and we tried to teach her the value of things. We wanted her to be inquisitive, hard-working and respectful of others, and I think we succeeded. She is also a secretive young woman, quite discreet, undoubtedly like me. She must have suffered sometimes from my absence and from our separation, although she never said anything to me.

My experience as a father brought me face to face with my doubts and my fears, possibly justified, that I would not be up to the job. Nevertheless, Léa has been lucky to have a loving mum who is devoted to her family and who bestowed all her time on her daughter and largely contributed to making her what she is today.

I tried to protect Léa and Annie from the brutality of competitive football, from the intensity of my disappointments, from the defeats (when I tended to shut myself away, silently analysing, stifling my anger to replace it with something more objective), but they still had to live with football and the central role it played in my life and they must have resented me for it sometimes. But I also tried to share the best with them, the values that I held dear. Annie and I are happy with and proud of the young woman that Léa has become.

The 1997–98 season was a winning one. I had settled in the club and I tried my utmost to fulfil my role of experienced manager and carry out the three missions I felt were essential. One: to have an impact on the result and the team's playing style. Two: to foster the players' individual development. Three: to strengthen the structure of the club and enhance its global influence. I was closely involved in the building of the new training centre, all the recruiting, the transfers, the daily coaching sessions and the work that each specialist was doing with the players. Of course, the important thing was the team's wonderful style based on the club's three fundamental values: *be together, act with class* and *move forward*. One way of living these values was to be classy on the pitch, on the bench and outside the club. In Japan, I had taken to wearing a suit and at Arsenal I never lost this habit. It was all about wanting to embody the club, make the supporters proud, respect the opponent and avoid sloppiness and settling for less, in everything we did. The players had understood the importance of holding themselves well, acting correctly and being as smart as possible. Other small apparently insignificant things mattered a lot: making a point of going to greet all the club's clients

153

and sponsors before each match, spending a while in the reception rooms and boardroom with them, decorating rooms with flowers in the opposing club's colours. It was a permanent quest for excellence and elegance.

It is also important to instil a performance culture. By this, I mean a culture that requires the leader and the players to ask themselves the fundamental questions that I have already mentioned:

How can I get better?

Have I achieved my full potential?

What can I do to get there?

These parameters are without doubt the key to any success. They help a player know himself better, identify his shortcomings, understand how to overcome them and reach the highest level. Those players had a balanced and remarkable mix of intelligence and motivation. I could count on men like Tony Adams, David Seaman, Lee Dixon, Ian Wright, Dennis Bergkamp, Marc Overmars, David Platt, Ray Parlour, and the French players I had brought over: Rémi Garde, Gilles Grimandi, Emmanuel Petit, Patrick Vieira and Nicolas Anelka.

It was an extraordinary season. From being a team in the middle of the table, we showed everyone that we could assert ourselves and be among the best. It was a generation of men who were motivated and hungry to win. But that was true throughout my twenty-two years at Arsenal, and it did not depend on whether or not we won titles. I was incredibly fond of all the players, and I deeply respected every one of them: their past history, their rigour, their strengths, the sacrifices they made to be the best.

That year we took on the huge challenge of winning the league title. I convinced myself we could win and I convinced the others that it was possible, too.

We were eight points behind Manchester United. On 14 March 1998, at Old Trafford, we won 1-0 with a goal from Marc Overmars, an outstanding player, from a decisive pass from Anelka. I had always been an admirer of Overmars' playing style. When I bought him he was coming out of recovery from a lengthy injury and many advised me against buying him. I went to see him play in Amsterdam and I could see he wasn't 100 per cent himself. But I was convinced that he was going to return to being the player he was, and I would be able to help him retrieve his best form. In terms of his style he was a decisive player, notably in his ability to call for the ball, and he analysed the game very well.

For me, this match was a turning point, a way of showing we were ready for the historic battle with Manchester United, that we could beat this exceptional team, and that the Premier League had us to reckon with.

Throughout all those years, I always enjoyed our rivalry with United, the tension at every match. Alex Ferguson was ready to die for his club, and I for mine. It was him or me. And this extreme rivalry can be explained by our competitiveness. Alex Ferguson was passionate about football, he was very capable and had crushing authority over English football because of his personality and the power of the club. He exerted a kind of subconscious pressure on everyone including the referees. For instance, time added on after injury time was even called Fergie time, and United used to win a lot at home with this additional time. His authority was primarily connected to the exceptional quality of the team.

There was always huge mutual respect, a classic rivalry. Of course there were many clashes, angry scenes between us, but this was not a game, it wasn't for show: it was our lives, our passion, our utter dedication to football. We were totally committed and thought only of victory. Obviously I knew that every sign of irritation I showed against him or his players was scrutinised, and that I needed to keep things under control. But sometimes controlling that tension is impossible. For one or the other of us, it boils over, and those are the moments the supporters and journalists remember. I knew we were very different, that he had a total hold over his club while at that time I was still more of a coach. I also recognised his huge qualities. He knew how to surround himself with the right people and didn't rest on his laurels when he was successful. He had a very effective, pragmatic approach that enabled him to eliminate anything that might prevent him from winning. He was an excellent man-manager who knew how to take the right

decisions and who showed acute psychological understanding. Our relationship was intense, with some stormy
periods and others that were calmer and more peaceful,
but it certainly livened up English football. That year we
won everything, and the following year, 1999, we lost the
FA Cup semi-final in extra time against Manchester United
and they won the Premiership title and the Champions
League. This shows how intense our rivalry was. The feeling
was that anything could happen, and that we had to work
doubly hard.

But when we won the title on 3 May, beating Everton 4-0,
on the penultimate weekend of the Premier League season,
we showed everyone and especially Manchester United
that we could beat them. And thirteen days later, when
we beat Newcastle 2-0 in the FA Cup final in the legendary
Wembley Stadium, it was wonderful. We knew that a big
adventure had only just begun. The double was wonderful
and intense.

I felt immensely proud for the team, for the club: this was
the fantastic response I was able to give to those who had
put their confidence in me, as well as those who had put
me through all those difficult weeks when I first arrived. It
was possible for an unknown foreign manager to gain the
trust of the team, to transform the habits of the players,
turn their lives upside down, win matches and most of all
win titles. But I wanted a lot more, and the successes of that
year gave me the clout, the credibility I had been hoping

for to be able to work harder, build even more of a winning team, give the club the best. I did not want just one title: we wanted to win everything.

In 1999, we didn't win the Premier League title. However, we made our mark in another way. We gave people something to remember us by, and we did it with style.

On 13 February, we were up against Sheffield United in the fifth round of the FA Cup. Alan Kelly, United's goalkeeper, kicked the ball out of play to allow the physios to treat an injured Lee Morris. But Nwankwo Kanu, who had just joined us from Inter Milan, took the ball and squared it for Overmars, who scored. The referee allowed the goal. We won, sparking huge scenes. We were all in the dressing room after the match. All the players agreed there should be a replay, as did the club chairman. We had to convince FIFA who were opposed to this because there had been no obvious error by the referee. Just twenty-four hours after the match was played, FIFA approved a replay. We had to win, and we did. It was a cup match, an important match that would take us to the semi-finals against Manchester United, but no one had any hesitation about replaying it, and for me, that was the most important thing. The famous *Act with class* that meant so much to us. It brought the team even closer and helped give the club, and me along with it, an even better image. These days, the idea of class and fair play tends to be ignored in favour of winning at any cost. Whoever does not come first or does not win the cup is left feeling they are nothing. But this is not true. God knows I like winning, but what we wanted was to win while respecting our values. I was awarded the fair play prize for this replay. I am very proud of that and I know the club was, too. Our previous victories along with this kind of gesture gave us a soul and a direction.

In order to build an even stronger team during those years, I brought in new players whose huge talent I could count on.

I already knew Thierry Henry, who had made his debut with me at Monaco. I knew him as a precocious, intelligent and brilliant player. He was playing at Juventus but it was not going well with his manager Carlo Ancelotti, who wanted to loan him out to another team and Thierry did not want to go. I sensed he was unhappy. I went over with David Dein to negotiate with Juventus. They hoped to get Anelka in exchange, but Anelka preferred Real Madrid. I waited for Nicolas to come and tell me himself that he wanted to go, and once he had done so we started negotiations with Real. I let him go but I was sad of course. I thought it was too early for him, that it would be too difficult to carry such a big transfer fee on his shoulders and that he was still in a learning phase. What counts the most in a player's career is the club he chooses and the moment he chooses it. I later felt Real did not give Nicolas as many chances as he should have had, that he was a bit sidelined, but there was nothing I could do.

We managed to bring Thierry Henry over and he arrived at the club in 1999. Very quickly, all the players and I saw that he had something special. I gradually got him playing more down the line. He had an extraordinary sense of timing when calling for the ball. At first, he was perhaps a little clumsy in his finishing and unsure of himself. He didn't think he could score. When you look back at his career today and you know he is the undisputed top goalscorer at Arsenal, the best striker in the club, that initial self-doubt might make people smile, but he needed to be taught to believe in himself, to find a way around his shyness, his nervousness, his fears, while at the same time knowing that his constant doubts also helped him to progress and be stronger. He was very quick at analysing everything that was going on and how he needed to react. This intelligence, this capacity to evaluate, understand and question oneself, is also the mark of great players. He immediately became part of the team, and was welcomed by his teammates who liked what he brought to the game. For everyone, for the fans and for us, he symbolised the golden age of Arsenal.

The following year, in 2000, I brought in Robert Pirès and Sylvain Wiltord.

Sylvain was playing at Bordeaux. I liked his mobility, his

availability, his opportunism and his teamwork. He was a team player and he knew how to take the right decision. I brought him in after a difficult negotiation. He had a reputation for being a bit wayward, like a wild animal. Rather than confronting things head on, he tended to avoid them. But with us, and subsequently at Lyon, he showed what an intelligent player he was. He had a real understanding of the game, an ability to create space, good ball reception, outstanding availability. He was a breath of fresh air to the team.

Robert Pirès was playing for Marseille. I had told their president, Robert Louis-Dreyfus, that I was interested in him. I knew that Pirès wanted to leave and I knew what he could bring to the team and to the big challenge I would shortly be presenting to the players. He was a fabulous player, world-class, and for a few years, before his injury, he was unquestionably the best left-midfielder in the world by far. He had incredible technique, he was smart, a finisher. He was a killer with a smile, the gentlest man in the world who would suddenly drive the ball exactly where it was needed. On 23 March 2002, we were playing Newcastle in an FA Cup sixth round replay, and he had an amazing start to the game. He scored in two minutes, but fell badly in a tackle and injured himself horribly. The doctors diagnosed a ruptured cruciate ligament and he needed an operation. It caused him huge distress, as it did me. I felt really bad for having played him, for not having left him to rest. I knew he would be unable to play for months or take part in that summer's World Cup, and that he ran the risk of never returning to top form again.

That year, on 8 May, we accomplished another feat: we beat Manchester United, on their pitch, with a goal from Sylvain Wiltord, and once again became Premier League champions. It was a huge victory, an unforgettable memory too, especially as four days previously we had beaten Chelsea 2-0 in the FA Cup final.

Those two victories against iconic Premier League clubs were highly symbolic and hugely meaningful for the fans and for us: we knew how to win trophies and cups, we could compete on the same level as clubs like Chelsea and Manchester United that had greater means and better financial resources than us. We had understood that we needed to compensate with the quality of our playing, and the quality of our recruitment, by knowing the market and taking an interest in players other than those who cost a lot to buy in.

*

The 2000s were an era when the team and the club opened up to an international structure. Whereas in 1998 the team had been culturally English, in the 2000s it was multicultural. I think it is possible for there to be several cultures, as long as it is not to the detriment of a common culture. And that's where a club culture comes in and is important. It has to be clear and accepted by everyone.

As part of my coaching style, I am always looking to progress, to become more accurate, fairer, stronger. In 2002, alongside my day job, I became acquainted with the work of TV sports commentating and it taught me a lot in unexpected ways.

I was contacted by Étienne Mougeotte and subsequently had a meeting with Charles Villeneuve, the head of sports at TF1, the French terrestrial TV channel. I was lucky enough to work alongside Jean-Michel Larqué, Thierry Roland, Thierry Gilardi and Christian Jeanpierre, who became a friend. Thanks to television, I was able to attend the big fixtures and travel to World Cups and major championships. It was another way of living my passion, and being in contact with players, managers and agents. And most of all, it allowed me to take a step back in all senses of the term: being positioned up high and looking down on the matches as an observer and commentator taught me a lot.

I instantly felt a very close connection with Christian Jeanpierre. Along with Bixente Lizarazu, there were three of us in the commentary box and I was the one who spoke the least. Three is probably one too many. I learnt from this experience: nowadays I could talk a lot more and would be more comfortable in the role. At the time, I didn't want to step on other people's toes, and I found it hard to give on-the-spot commentary, in the thick of the action. I prefer the pre- and post-analysis that I now do for BeIN Sports. In fact, in 2004, I signed my first contract with Nasser al-Khelaifi, who was then head of sports at BeIN and would rapidly climb the ladder there. Of course, I am a man with practical experience: I prefer the competition, the action and putting ideas into practice rather than just playing with ideas. But I liked trying to explain to the viewers what football is, what the game is, and we know that words do count and can change many things, that talking is important. A manager, as I have often said, is a man with clear ideas, who knows what he wants and expresses it clearly. Commentating on matches and analysing for large audiences helped me to clarify my thinking and to communicate it to others. That was also where I gauged the extent to which television would become involved in football, that it would provide football with considerable income but in exchange would be increasingly present, and would demand new services. I realised it was the club chairmen, not the technical staff, who would be approached for these services, and that we would have to accept this and try to make the best of it while protecting the team and trying to set limits.

*

In 2001–02, not only did we win the Premiership title, we did so without losing an away match all season. It was then that the press began to dub us 'the Invincibles' after the famous Preston North End side that won the league and cup double in 1889 without suffering a single defeat. I really believed that that year our performance and consistency marked a genuine shift of power in the fierce rivalry with Manchester United, and I challenged my players to aim to emulate Preston's historic feat and win the league without losing a match.

The following season, 2002–03, started well. To prove to the players that I had confidence in them, that I was confident myself, I made an announcement at a press conference: we can win the title without losing. And never mind those who called us crazy or arrogant. I'd always thought a manager's ultimate goal was to win a championship without losing a game. It was a kind of obsession I carried around with me. You can be top of the class with 90 per cent, but you can't be second with 100 per cent.

Of course with every game unbeaten the pressure on us to achieve this feat was increasing. We extended our run of unbeaten games to thirty in October, a Premier League record, before losing at Everton to a last-minute goal by a sixteen-year-old Wayne Rooney. With that defeat the pressure was lifted but so was the aura of invincibility, and it was hard to match the incredibly high standard and level of consistency we had set for ourselves. Though we eventually finished runners-up to United I felt that we were very close to pulling it off again, to beating our great rivals and leaving our mark on football history. I felt the team was unified, experienced, powerful, playing at top form, with a positive mental attitude, a combination of older players who loved competition and solid young players who had everything to prove and a life ahead of them. There was not much to choose between the strengths of the two sides. All it needed was a touch of magic here and there, perhaps a modicum of luck, and it would fall into place. We had won the FA Cup again in Cardiff, 1-0 against Southampton with a Robert Pirès goal, and I asked my players why we hadn't won the title. They told me I was putting too much pressure on them, that the goal of winning the Premier League without losing a match seemed unachievable to them.

I believed they could do even better next season, so when the players reassembled after the summer break I reiterated the challenge: win without losing a match and become the modern-day Invincibles. That has always been a lesson for me: setting the highest ambition and believing in it, sowing the seeds one year and harvesting two years later.

'There was fierce but respectful rivalry among the players, they set themselves goals and were prepared to pay the price for them. We experienced a kind of collective state of grace. Individually, each of them also had strong charisma and personal ambitions. They kept up this level of expectation throughout the whole season, and I admire that very much.'

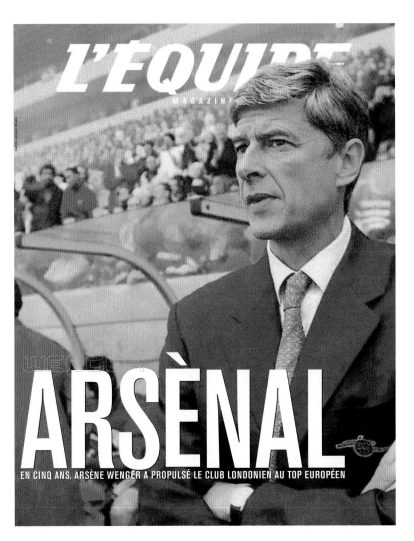

PHOTO: HUGUES FÉVRIER

ARSÈNAL

EN CINQ ANS, ARSÈNE WENGER A PROPULSÉ LE CLUB LONDONIEN AU TOP EUROPÉEN

'Arsenal. In five years Arsène Wenger has propelled the London club to the summit of Europe.' A *L'Équipe* article from April 2001.

With captain Patrick Vieira and our three trophies from 2002 – the FA Cup, Premier League trophy and the Community Shield.

Winning the Premier League at Old Trafford in 2002 was particularly satisfying. Celebrating are Sylvain Wiltord, scorer of the game's only goal, and Lauren.

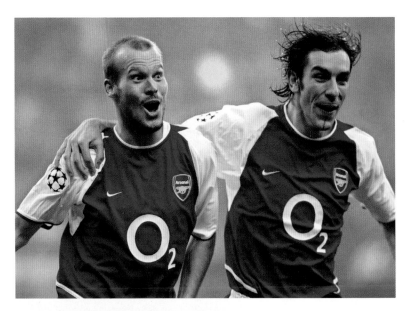

Above After a 0-3 home defeat to Inter Milan, hammering them 5-1 in Milan in November 2003 was one of our greatest triumphs. Freddie Ljungberg, scorer of the second goal, celebrates with Robert Pirès, scorer of the fifth.

Above left Thierry Henry wheels away after his second goal of the night.

Left Edu and Sol Campbell tracking Inter Milan's Christian Vieri, scorer of their only goal.

Left Celebrating Arsenal winning the Premier League after the match against Spurs at White Hart Lane in April 2004.

Below left The Invincibles on a victorious ride through Highbury and Islington, with David Dein and Pat Rice on the right of the picture.

Right Giving instructions to Thierry Henry at the Bernabeu where his wonderful goal gave us a 1-0 victory over Real Madrid in the first leg in February 2006.

Saluting the supporters

Left In winter, in a state of despair . . .

Below With Thierry Henry, the club's greatest-ever goalscorer

Right With Cesc Fàbregas, the club's youngest-ever player and a future captain

Below Disappointment after the Champions League final in Paris in 2006.

The last match at Highbury, 7 May 2006, a 4-2 win over Wigan

7

THE INVINCIBLES

At the start of the 2003–04 season, I repeated to the players what I had declared earlier: they could win the title without losing. I believed in it, and it was our goal.

I remember every single player in that exceptional team. Obviously, everyone remembers the stars, the players who were the lynchpins: Patrick Vieira, Gilberto Silva, Ray Parlour, Freddie Ljungberg, Robert Pirès, Dennis Bergkamp, Thierry Henry, Lauren, Jens Lehmann and Ashley Cole, who had been at the academy since he was eleven and had debuted with me at Arsenal. There were also two defenders who were fundamentally important.

Sol Campbell arrived at Arsenal in 2001. He had been the

mainstay at our north London rivals Tottenham, where his contract with the club was about to expire. No one could have imagined for a single second that he would come to us. To prepare for his arrival, and to discuss conditions, we used to meet at David Dein's house at around 11 o'clock at night and walk around the neighbourhood, talking until midnight, 1 o'clock in the morning. Only David, Sol, his agent Sky Andrew and I knew what was going on. We were gauging the impact it would have. When I called a press conference to announce the arrival of a new player, and Sol Campbell walked into the room full of journalists, it was a bombshell. Joining us after so many years at Spurs was an outstanding act of courage. And what we feared, knowing the supporters, their passion, their fury, came to pass: he often had a difficult life in London, having to deal with banners calling him a traitor, a Judas. For me, he was a man who had great qualities, an outstanding defender with phenomenal power. He had an enormous impact in the five seasons he was with us and the club would not have been at all the same without him. But I know what he had to endure to play for Arsenal, the pressure of the incessant attacks.

There is, of course, a historic rivalry between Arsenal and Tottenham Hotspur. To begin with, Arsenal was a south London club that set up in the north of the city, near Tottenham's territory. More than any other match in the season, the week before a game against Tottenham was unlike any other week within the club. From the Monday onwards, the tension and nerves would be at their most taut. I was more removed. I had come from abroad, but I could still sense this tension very clearly. Anyone who had endured this traditional rivalry would realise that for this one week everybody would be on alert, as if the air-raid sirens could sound at any time. In short, it was more than a mere football match played between two teams of eleven. Within north London families, those who supported Arsenal and those who supported Tottenham would not speak to one another over that weekend. My assistant Pat Rice was tempted to select only the fighters – but it was always the technicians that allowed us to win, such as Robert Pirès or Thierry Henry. It was important to stay totally Zen in regard to that state of tension.

The zenith (or nadir) of this competitiveness between the two clubs was when we played our first match against Tottenham with Sol in our team. He had been a legendary Spurs player, and there were never-ending shouts of 'Judas!' from Tottenham fans. After these derby matches, there were frequently brawls in the street. It was difficult to get out of the stadium when we were leaving White Hart Lane. A game lost to Spurs left us in a terrible state for several days afterwards. It is just as well we didn't lose very many. I think there is less of that tension today: the stakes are no longer the same.

Next to Sol, I played Kolo Touré, who arrived a year later.

He had been trained by the Jean-Marc Guillou Academy in the Ivory Coast. Jean-Marc, whom I knew from my time at AS Cannes and Monaco, had left France to settle in West Africa and had founded this football academy in the Ivorian capital Abidjan with the help of his friends, including me. It was an important school for African football. As a result, Jean-Marc, with his immense qualities as a coach, trained a whole generation of players in the Ivory Coast and neighbouring countries. I always followed his work, I knew his preparation of players was excellent; the working environment he provided enabled them to achieve a high technical standard. The Academy no longer exists but Jean-Marc created similar structures with the same demanding standard in Mali, Algeria and elsewhere. We established a partnership between the club and the Academy, and that's how I spotted this player and others after him, such as Emmanuel Eboué, who joined us the following year.

Kolo Touré had come over for trials at Basel, Bastia and Strasbourg. And they all rejected him. He was due to return to the Ivory Coast, but he was a player who intrigued me. I wanted to see him play, and I trusted Jean-Marc, even though I knew that players needed to learn how to cope with the European game and this was a real test for them. I offered him a trial. And I saw: he was as hungry as a wolf, he was ready to consume and demolish everyone. I kept him. He became a pivotal player in the Invincibles, a key man, and the cheapest in the entire history of football as I had negotiated his contract for a derisory sum. He became one of the best central defenders in any league.

This outstanding defence also featured Lauren, a top-quality Cameroonian player who was built for fighting and had been a midfield player before I moved him to full-back. He was an interesting player to coach, because he became very involved and had a great technical capacity. He had played in the Africa Cup of Nations in 2000 (when he was Player of the Tournament) and in 2002. I had bought him from Real Mallorca, and it was a great buy for the club.

And of course Ashley Cole, who would go on to have a brilliant career. He was a real red-and-white player. He had grown up in the club from the age of eleven. From his first match, he showed he had the form, that he was not intimidated. He continued to show the courage and the capacities he had demonstrated at the outset. It is one of the great regrets of my life that I lost him to Chelsea, thanks to a misunderstanding in the negotiations with his agent.

Our goalkeeper Jens Lehmann was a man with an unrivalled will to win. He had been awarded UEFA Club Goalkeeper of the Year in 1996–97 and was to receive that accolade again in 2005–06. He had been shown more red cards at Borussia Dortmund than any other player in the club's history, but I saw something special in him.

So we had put in place a superb defence that was one of the drivers of our success, the nerve-centre of the war of the Invincibles.

*

So, at the start of the season, I was convinced we now had everything in place to fulfil my ambition for the club. I wanted the team to be convinced also, to internalise the challenge: we had already won matches, championships, trophies, and now we could achieve something even bigger. When setting lofty objectives, it takes time and patience for them to become fixed in people's minds. But my aim was to win all the time, to defer defeat and make the fear of losing disappear.

And we did better than winning the championship without losing: 49 matches in a row without defeat. Throughout all these months, stretching from May 2003 to October 2004, we kept our motivation and our spirit intact as we worked relentlessly. We were solely focused on the objective of playing very well during every match, swiftly correcting any individual faults, maintaining the level of our ambition.

We had all endeavoured to develop a unique spirit specific to that particular team. A performance culture. Each player had to have a clear picture of areas that needed improving. This was the moment the team really integrated the values I felt were important: suddenly, my project became theirs and they ran with it for 49 matches. There was fierce but respectful rivalry among the players, they set themselves goals and were prepared to pay the price for them. We experienced a kind of collective state of grace.

Individually, each of them also had strong charisma and personal ambitions. They kept up this level of expectation throughout the whole season, and I admire that very much. Because a team can't be protected against everything for a whole season. The players must have had worries, aches and pains, but when they played, they were there only for the game, the team, their passion. Those players did better than others because they really made our project, our desire, their own, developing their own style which became the Arsenal style, relying on what will always make a team successful: individual talent, collective intelligence and humility.

I remember that everything was important at that time, everything had to function to put us in a state of mind where all we thought about was the game, and winning. I had rituals, I always prepared in the same way: sport in the morning, preparation with the players, everything followed a pre-ordained pattern! I had my coffee at the same time, we all ate together, put ourselves in match conditions, I chaired the pre-match meeting, we had the walk, the stretching session. All this allowed me to feel the team's energy through the players' attitudes, concentration levels and capacity to listen.

During that time, I discovered something wonderful: we were no longer afraid of defeat. And with that fear removed, we could be better. We concentrated solely on what could make us win. And so I discovered another aspect of the job that I really loved and that made me even more passionate about it. Every day we had to become even more resolute about maintaining our shared expectations.

We became Premier League champions five matches before the end of the season. But I did not want us to stop with that win. I thought we should maintain our effort, our expectations, and that this dream of a life without defeat should continue. I congratulated them for the win but said it was not enough: that they could, we could, become immortal by continuing to win. They hung on until the 50th match, and they certainly know it now: they are immortal. That was the reward for staying resolute, concentrating on the work required, and keeping that amazing sense of all being in it together. At the start of each match, Campbell would shout 'Together!' as a rallying cry, which says it all about our team spirit.

I often relive those 49 undefeated matches. I do believe in signs to a certain extent, and as I was born in 1949, I sometimes tell myself it was our destiny to lose the 50th. Those 49 matches are etched within me and within each player: it is something fundamental, a triumph born of passion. I subsequently had other teams who could have won like that but were missing something. It is often through comparison that we can gauge the quality of players, their intelligence, and also the luck that we had. Defeat comes from a stupid mistake and a bit of selfishness. What has left the biggest mark on me today is those players who had the capacity to work in the collective interest because they were motivated by the desire to win. Always attaching importance to real priorities is certainly the mark of great people. And this was also the approach we took at our meetings to prepare for a match.

On 24 October 2004, after all those incredible matches, our first defeat came against Manchester United. It's a match I will never forget. We lost 2-0 and it felt like a real hold-up job. It was a hard match, with lots of duels, fouls, frayed tempers. We dominated without managing to score. And then, in the 73rd minute, the referee gave a penalty for a foul by Sol Campbell that was undeserved and that changed the whole match. And from there, everything started drifting, the start of a downward spiral. The players and I felt it was hugely unfair. We did not deserve to lose. After the match, the players were shoving one another, the managers too; Alex Ferguson was in the middle of the mêlée and one player, Cesc Fàbregas, threw a slice of pizza that hit him on his head. Clearly, our defeat, the very generous penalty, the fights and the pizza meant that the match went down in the history of our stormy relationship with Manchester United. But it was a heavy blow for me and the team. We knew that the good times were over; that unique moment, the time without fear, had passed, and we knew it would be hard to recapture that state of grace. We were so disappointed that we could only draw our next two games against sides who would both go on to be relegated. And though we followed that with victory in a crazy north London derby by the odd goal in nine at White Hart Lane, we generally felt flat and drew or lost far too often. Everyone found it hard to get back on their feet.

A few months later, another match left its mark on the world of English football: it was 14 February 2005, Arsenal–Crystal Palace, 5-1. The press noticed that the Arsenal team had not one English player. (Ashley Cole and Sol Campbell were not playing.) There was Dennis Bergkamp, José Antonio Reyes, Kolo Touré, Thierry Henry, Patrick Vieira, Lauren . . . But I didn't realise this when I chose the players. The journalists' reaction and the resulting controversy did of course surprise me, even though I knew that they were sensitive to their readers' fears for the health of the English game on the international stage. At the time, there were not enough top-quality players; the level of the Premier League was very good but there was no pool of young native talent. But I would argue that young players tend to want to emulate the foreign stars that they see in training and performing on the pitch, and this helps them to progress in their own development. The criticism was unjustified.

Nowadays, the quality of the English league has improved, young players have progressed, notably thanks to the excellent academies flourishing everywhere. The English have created quality structures with fantastic coaches and a very high coaching standard, whereas before youngsters trained at school as best they could, in conditions that were similar to amateur ones. The FA's restructuring of the training of young players has born rich dividends in the recent success of England youth sides at international age-group tournaments.

Today, there is a pool of young talent from England and all over the world, and the standard is very high. It took time, and we contributed to this. The Arsenal academy recruited young players from abroad. I thought that by getting them when they were young, they would more quickly and easily absorb the way the Premier League worked, the English mentality and culture, and that they would inspire English players. So when these young foreign recruits started playing, they had already been in England for four years and no one could accuse them of not knowing or understanding the English game. And I was sure that opening up in this way would contribute to Arsenal's success, that a combination of local and foreign culture was needed, that we could bring in the better players without worrying about what passport they had and hence contribute to raising the level of the English game. In 2005, that created controversy and a torrent of criticism. But I will argue with anybody who says we damaged the English game with our youth recruitment policy. For me, all that counted was the quality of the men, and I will always defend this idea against any tendency to be inward-looking.

Sport has an extraordinary social responsibility. It can be ahead of society and set an example to follow. That is its role. It is the only activity that is based solely on merit, that rewards merit alone. I have always felt that this was a very big responsibility, and one must prove equal to the task. Which is why attention paid to the academies is of prime importance. If an academy is effective, well structured, well thought-out, ambitious, with a clear strategy and strong values, it enables talents to emerge and integrate into the first team. And I repeat: no matter where those young talents come from, all that counts is the effort a player is prepared to make, his gifts, his passion and his work.

I do not think there is a rise in racism in English football. I do not get the impression there is racism within the clubs I have known best. On the fringes and in the outside world, yes, of course it exists. Our players have been insulted and racially abused on occasion – Patrick Vieira and Sol Campbell, for example. But inside the clubs today, and rightfully so, there are things we no longer accept. Our resistance to racism and our refusal to accept it has become stronger. We have not yet found the best way to punish racism and violence by some so-called 'supporters'. Should a club be compelled to forfeit or lose a match because of two or three crazy or delinquent fans? One way is the use of video-cameras in each stadium to help identify the guilty and exclude them permanently from all stadiums.

What makes training young players successful is, first, the recruitment, second, the player's personal development programme and third, his integration into the first team. These days, training academies in England are very effective in the first two and much less so in the third.

Talented players are spotted very young and specialise so early, so they can become increasingly isolated and cut off from a normal social life. And those around them, especially their families for whom they represent hope and a major investment, have high expectations for their success. By setting out to create an environment that favours a player's development, the club creates a situation of permanent support. The challenge today is to find a better balance between support and individual initiative. The training of a top athlete should enable him or her to develop their judgement of situations and their capacity to overcome major disappointments.

Through personality tests that we carried out with Jacques Crevoisier over a ten-year period, we realised that enduring motivation is the determining factor in a player's success. Young people need role models in order to learn. They need to have one strong attribute to succeed. You build your life, your career, based on one dominant attribute: you never have them all.

If football can be summed up as ball reception, decision-making and the quality of the performance, we realised that the factor that makes the difference between players is the ability to take in information. In the Premier League, the good player takes in around four to six pieces of information in the ten seconds prior to receiving the ball, and the very good player takes in eight to ten pieces of information. It is therefore important to develop exercises that help increase this ability to gather information.

In my career as a professional manager, I have often faced criticism, and I have tried to be as fair as possible and take on board the criticisms that are justified. But I have always stood my ground when it comes to my deeply held convictions about the game. I've had to make decisions that have provoked strong reactions, opposition, but I had the maturity to deal with this. And I've sought to do things my way, to work without compromising too much on what I believe in and to promote a free-flowing style of football. The flip side, of course, is accepting the brutality of the repercussions and the loneliness that comes from being the one who has the rigour required to make the tough decisions. This profession leaves no room for sloppiness, and there is a heavy price to be paid for the slightest wavering. Nothing counted except the game and the club. It is in this sense too that football could be, or should remain, a template for society: more fairness and more reward for whoever puts in the most effort. Top-level sport is based on this principle and can serve as an example through the demands it places on people. The lives of great players are built on their passion, their talent, their merit, their investment. And they are role models. That is one of the reasons we love and admire them. We have a bit too much of an image of hugely privileged men with big cars, expensive watches and beautiful women, but that was not the football I knew and loved at Arsenal for all those years. One thing we don't show enough is the efforts these players have made to get where they are; it's not said often enough that they are only 20, 22 years old and at that age everyone does foolish things, but other people don't get into the papers because of them. Whenever that happened, my role as manager was to carry on respecting the individual players and simply remind them of their responsibilities, the example they should set.

Despite the controversy in 2005, it seems to me that today everyone accepts that those foreign players were role models, and recognises how they made the club strong, proving in every match their love for our game, for Arsenal, for the Premier League, for winning.

Throughout all those years, I was guided by and shielded from the criticism, the challenges and the adversity by an unwavering determination. This willpower protected me from fear: it made me act by listening only to what I was passionate about. At Arsenal, I discovered that being a manager was a bit like Russian roulette: before each match you put a bullet in the barrel, during the match you squeeze the trigger, and you hope and believe that you won't take the bullet.

There were a lot of matches that made me feel that way. In particular, the FA Cup final on 21 May 2005 against Manchester United that we won on a penalty shootout. It was the last time Patrick Vieira kicked a ball to win a match for us, before he left Arsenal for Juventus. We won, but United played an outstanding game. I had managed to convince Vieira to stay an extra year and not go to Real. He listened to me; he wanted to leave on a final wonderful experience and that Cup final match gave him what he wanted. It is a magical memory for everyone, and part of my unique record never equalled by any manager since: winning seven FA Cups and seven Charity and Community Shields!

'I had accepted that we would lose those star players who wanted to leave; I knew I couldn't hold them back. It was very difficult, of course, but we had decided to keep our finances under control. We had committed to the construction of a new stadium, we had to be careful, and I had also decided to pursue a policy of bringing in young players.'

8

LEAVING HIGHBURY, BUILDING EMIRATES

I instinctively sensed that the 2004–05 season, crowned with victories, and that FA Cup win in particular, signalled the end of an era. In the years that followed, we had to deal with and accept the departure of some iconic players: first, Vieira, the following year Henry, and then Pirès, all players who had done so much for my credibility and who had put all their talent and spirit to the service of the club. And then we had to cope with our planned, but nevertheless painful, departure from the legendary Highbury stadium to the Emirates. All this happening at the same time inevitably created upheaval and readjustment, and although those years may have been perceived as more difficult than

191

previous ones, they also gave rise to new challenges and new talents to nurture.

I had accepted that we would lose those star players who wanted to leave; I knew I couldn't hold them back. It was very difficult, of course, but we had decided to keep our finances under control. We had committed to the construction of a new stadium, we had to be careful, and I had also decided to pursue a policy of bringing in young players – the long-standing players knew this. Thierry Henry had come to see me: 'Coach, I'm 31 years old, we can't win the championship with the young players.' I understood what he meant: it was going to take time to build a team that was as solid and experienced as the one in which he'd been so influential and, at 31, he was in a hurry, he still wanted other major victories. I couldn't hold him back, nor could I say to players who had given their all to the club: 'No, you will not leave.' I also knew their departure was a way of bringing money into the club to pay for the new stadium. That was why my experience of those departures was different from the supporters': I couldn't hold a grudge against the players, and I knew that departures were part of the job. Players are pros, they want to win. You need to be philosophical and always put yourself in their shoes; and when somebody has given their all, and you can no longer fulfil their very legitimate ambitions, you cannot be angry. Vieira left for Juventus, Henry for Barça, Pirès for Villarreal. But all these players will forever be associated with Arsenal, they will always be Arsenal players first and foremost.

For a football club, it's the technical part that is the most important, that's the real crux of the matter. Directors do not always accept this. If you change the commercial director, that doesn't change the club. But if Thierry Henry leaves, a new story begins. Football hinges on the players, on their qualities. Nowadays, men and the modern world would have us believe that players are interchangeable, but that is not true. When you lose a Vieira, a Pirès, an Henry, they cannot be replaced. You cannot hold them back financially, and besides, age is a key and unavoidable factor: those players were going to leave in any case and would not have been able to play for much longer. The technical side is constantly forced to evolve. And so begins another story that tries to preserve and transmit the values and spirit of the club and ensure that it endures.

This new story that was unfolding for the club, for the team and for me included the construction of the new stadium.

On 7 May 2006, we played our last game at Highbury. We were playing against Wigan Athletic and we won 4-2 with a goal from Pirès and a hat-trick from Thierry Henry, including one from a penalty. Despite being 2-1 down at half-time, we pulled it off. It was very emotional, particularly for those hugely iconic players who knew they were soon going to leave the club. We had organised a farewell ceremony, and The Who's frontman, Roger Daltrey, an Arsenal fan, performed a special valedictory song he had composed. I was very sad, there in that stadium where I'd experienced so many emotions in such exceptional circumstances. Years after leaving Highbury, and even to this day, I sometimes drive past the stadium, alone in my car. The four stands were converted into apartment blocks. The windows of the apartments look out not onto the street but onto a garden, our former stadium; I thought about buying one, but it would have been much too sad. In order to build the new stadium, we had a constant need for money, and converting Highbury into apartments was a way of financing the Emirates project. We had become the biggest property company in England at that moment in time. When the property crisis hit London in 2008, we struggled to sell the apartments and the situation was extremely critical, forcing us at times to sell at a discount and use the money earned from football to finance the property company. Then the crisis blew over, we sold the apartments and the neighbouring land that also belonged to us, and we recovered from those difficult times.

It was heart-breaking to leave Highbury behind and watch as it vanished. We had no choice: the stadium held 38,000 spectators and we had a huge waiting list for every match. The old stadium was no longer sufficient. We were like a company that had to turn down clients. After looking for land nearby, we chose to build elsewhere. We took out a loan amounting to £260 million to fund the project: it ended up costing £390 million. The land on which we decided to build cost £128 million alone. And a number of companies and a waste recycling plant had to be relocated. Then the cost of the stadium shot up. At the time that the stadium was built, each seat cost £4,000. And the new stadium had a capacity of just over 60,000.

We became dependent on the banks. This long-term investment project was important to undertake for the club, but it also brought major constraints. The banks demanded guarantees such as restricting salaries to 50 per cent of the overall budget. And they sought a technical guarantee by asking me to sign up for five years. The project and I were interconnected. That committed me over the long term. I had just spent ten years at Arsenal and I was signing up for a five-year term full of pitfalls. I must admit I was very happy to do so. I remember saying to Annie that I would probably stop when I was 50. In the end, the adventure ended when I was 69 years old. It was no sacrifice for me as I had lost none of my passion for the club. I loved working as hard as I did and contributing to making Arsenal a modern club with a structure suited to the way modern football works. With the stadium, I was able to fully accomplish what I also felt to be the role of a manager: adding another dimension to a club. And I had the incredible luck to be able to do all that over time.

On that day in May 2006, when we said farewell to

Highbury, I was not thinking about what we would accomplish later: most of all, I was sad but also grateful for all the joy I had experienced in this stadium. I had to say goodbye to what I thought of as my home. Highbury had a particular feel, the spirit of those who had gone before us and the spirit we had tried to give it. I felt this powerfully, and I knew that when we lost this stadium, we would never completely find this spirit elsewhere. It was a bit like comparing one of those old houses that is no longer fit for purpose, but where we feel totally at home even though the heating does not work properly, with an ultramodern, practical house where we always feel a bit like an outsider. Yet I like the Emirates, I know it had to be built, that this stadium and the resources it generates were necessary for the club's future financial potential. Today the Emirates is the club's natural home and I am proud of it. For all that, anyone who knew Highbury will always be nostalgic like me, a feeling future generations probably won't experience. I know the supporters have also had a difficult and contradictory relationship with the new stadium, because they knew that throughout all those years while it was being built and costing us money, we had to rein in our ambitions. Once again, the future belongs to the next generations, the page has turned and today, with extremely healthy finances and renewed ambition, the supporters are proud of their stadium.

*

Ten days after the emotional farewell to Highbury, we played Barcelona in the Champions League final in the Stade de France in Paris. It was a crucial moment, the climax of so much effort for the players. We had previously eliminated Real Madrid, Juventus and Villarreal in style.

Before my arrival, I think that Arsenal had only played twice in the European Cup (in 1971–72 and 1991–92) and never in its successor, the Champions League. My objective was this final. Little by little, with a lot of hard work, season after season, we established ourselves in the competition. We qualified nineteen times in a row, we went out at the group stage on a regular basis, we fought, we reached the quarter-finals, the semi-finals and then we made it to the final. The Champions League brought the club a great deal of recognition. This is less the case today; it's almost harder to win the English Premier League than the Champions League. Throughout those years, Europe was dominated by Real, Barça and Bayern. Whatever we did, because of the draw, we always ended up against one or other of the big three.

I played eight FA Cup finals and won seven, but I have always had a kind of European curse. I have always lost the Champions League in unbelievable circumstances, and these are matches that will always stick in my throat. But the one that hurts the most and that I've never been able to watch again since is the match in the 2006 final against Barça. Throughout the knock-out phase of the competition, we did not concede a single goal. In the round of 16, we were up against Real, who had some incredible players: Zidane, Ronaldo, Roberto Carlos, Beckham, Raúl. We won the away leg and drew at home. In the quarter-finals, we were up against Juve where Trezeguet, Vieira, Ibrahimović, Emerson, Thuram and Buffon played. We won 2-0 at home, and held them to a goalless draw in Turin. In the semi-finals, we took on Villarreal: Kolo Touré secured the win for us in the first leg at home, and in the return leg, Lehmann saved us by making a string of fine saves and saving a penalty in the last minute. Sport always has surprises in store, and sudden reversals of fortune, and the drama and irony is that Lehmann got us into the final, but will always regret the foul that got him sent off in the 18th minute. It is his worst memory, but it was not his fault. He was sent off. We were playing in a Champions League final and we found ourselves down to ten men at the start of the match. Some difficult decisions had to be taken quickly. So I substituted Robert Pirès in the 20th minute to make way for the replacement goalkeeper Manuel Almunia, and I know that this provoked incomprehension and anger in Robert, but the situation required it. We were going to have to defend and play on the counter-attack. He was 32 years old, he had just had a major operation, and even though he was still an outstanding player, he was no longer the Pirès of 2002. As cruel as it was, and indeed it was, I had to do it. And I had to make an instant decision, because in our profession, one has to react fast. Despite us being down to ten men, Sol Campbell opened the scoring in the 37th minute, after heading in a free-kick. But in the second half, Samuel Eto'o and Juliano Belletti both scored, in the 76th and 80th minutes, and we lost. It is an awful memory and I am still enormously frustrated about it to this day. Obviously, alongside the departure of certain players and the change of stadium, it left its mark on that year, the end of an era.

Victory in the Champions League would have been a wonderful end to the adventure of the Invincibles, rewarding all the efforts made by the players and the club during the construction of the new stadium. The adventure remains unfinished. Arsenal have never yet managed to win the Champions League, but I know that the club is now in a position to do so: it is once again in the best possible financial situation, it must now take the best decisions regarding the technical side. If regret is the distance between what I would have liked to happen and what actually happened, I obviously have huge regrets in this case. But I now know that we would have had to win the Premiership and every other competition every year in order to have no regrets at all. You regret losing one player more than another, you regret a particular decision, you regret a technical error that was not corrected properly, you regret something you should have said at half-time and did not. Even today, I still have this need to question myself in order to progress.

That final was a real blow to me personally. In 2006, we moved into our new stadium and we had to leave that defeat behind us and face many challenges. That required courage and total commitment from everyone.

On 9 August 2006, we inaugurated the Emirates Stadium with the first match of the season, against Aston Villa. It was a new era.

I knew we had no room for manoeuvre financially. We were going to have to cut our costs, watch every single penny and at the same time play against clubs who had even more money than before. It was the most critical and most dangerous period, leaving the club extremely exposed. For seven years, we would have to concentrate on survival, managing the club with the utmost rigour and getting the best out of the team. Paradoxically, it was during this period, when results were more difficult to come by, that I was working the hardest, putting aside my personal ambitions as I was receiving offers from many other clubs and declining them all, even the most tempting ones. Juventus, Real Madrid, PSG contacted me, Bayern, France, England . . . With hindsight, all in all, I am happy to have been able to say no to more glory, more money, and to have been guided only by the idea of loyally serving the club during that period. Most of all – and anyone who is an Arsenal supporter will understand this – I had knitted myself a soul in red and white.

A relaxed moment on the bench

Meeting the Queen, with club chairman Peter Hill-Wood
(on my right) and long-serving director Ken Friar.

At the construction site, and *(below)* then
in the completed Emirates stadium

The new Emirates stadium which we moved to in July 2006.

Sent to the stands at Old Trafford to join the Manchester United fans after an altercation with the referee in November 2009.

Sir Alex and I were serious and active rivals for sixteen years.

After our 3-2 victory in the FA Cup Final at Wembley against
Hull in 2014. You can see Bacary Sagna, Olivier Giroud,
Per Mertesacker, Thomas Vermaelen, Mathieu Flamini
and Mikel Arteta, now the head coach.

I was drenched in champagne!

After our 2-1 triumph against Chelsea in the 2017 final . . .

. . . and celebrating our victory

My final home game against Burnley, a 5-0 victory on 6 May 2018

Time to say farewell

'Thanks, Arsene. We'll miss you too.'

'Those financial restraints, compared to clubs that lived solely on credit, that absolute determination not to spend 200 when we were only making 100, which suited my character and philosophy, taught me a great deal.'

9

MY LIFE AT ARSENAL, A NEW ERA

In 2007–08, we were top of the league for three-quarters of the season but we cracked in early spring with successive draws against Birmingham City, Aston Villa and Wigan. We finished behind Manchester United and Chelsea, on 83 points.

To pay back the money we owed for the Emirates, we had to qualify for the Champions League three times out of five, and we needed an annual average gate of 54,000 per match. We were in the Champions League five times out of five, and averaged 60,000 spectators per match. Some years, in April, when I thought we wouldn't make it, that we wouldn't qualify, I couldn't sleep at all, I was extremely tense and, when we got to the last match of the season, I would sing as if we had actually won the league championship. More than anyone, I knew how crucial it was for the club, and I promised myself we would do enough to qualify.

We qualified for the Champions League nineteen consecutive times. Only Real Madrid with twenty have exceeded this between 1997 and 2017. It's true that, for us, it was sometimes a close-run thing that was decided in the final matches. But we won the Premiership three times, came second six times, third five times and fourth on six occasions, which is proof of how remarkably consistent we were. Little by little, year by year, we managed to repay our debts and build some great teams. We were just lacking the financial appeal and the experience of some great players. And paradoxical as this might sound, especially to the journalists who tended to focus on the Invincibles era, these were wonderful years. The players were young, very young, players like Cesc Fàbregas, the youngest player in the club's history, to whom I gave his debut at the age of sixteen; Jack Wilshere, the youngest Arsenal player to make his debut in the league in 2008, also at the age of sixteen; and Samir Nasri, who also made his debut in the team in 2008, when he was 21 years old. Nevertheless, they were surrounded by very talented and experienced players like Alexander Hleb, William Gallas and Tomáš Rosický.

A player is not the same and doesn't offer the same to

the team between the ages of 16 and 22 as he does between 24 and 28. It is this level of maturity, experience and clear-headedness that we were lacking in the big matches. We lost those matches on small details that were always related to a want of experience. However, this was the route we needed to take in order to build the club of the future and make a new start on healthy foundations. With our colossal bank debts, we were less able to buy players: this is why we turned to young ones, while other clubs, which had artificial resources and existed on external sponsorship, clubs like Chelsea, Manchester United and Manchester City, had huge financial clout and could buy whomever they wanted, often even our players. That was also difficult, but I had prepared for that: we had to stay within our budget no matter what, keep to our financial commitments. Our budget was strictly managed and, whenever we bought a player, we negotiated his salary hard. We had to make sure our payroll did not exceed 50 per cent of the club's budget. The only cash we had available was the money that was freed up by transfers when we made a good sale. And that was all. But with less money we were still effective, and that for me was key: in a tough league, we were always competitive enough to finish in the top four. With hindsight, those financial restrictions, compared to clubs that lived solely on credit, that absolute determination not to spend 200 when we were only making 100, which suited my character and philosophy, taught me a great deal. And it seemed fair:

we had chosen to undertake an ambitious development project for the club, and that inevitably had consequences.

Another factor was that numerous players, and the younger ones in particular, experienced some terrible injuries. For some of them, it put a stop to their careers, for others it certainly hindered them a great deal, especially if they were out of action for a long time. They are one of the great regrets of my life, those major injuries. I gave many young players their debut when they were sixteen or seventeen. It is an age when they are vulnerable, both physically and tactically, in that they have a tendency to head straight into dangerous situations and not know how to protect themselves, charging into some perilous duels. Aaron Ramsey, Jack Wilshere, Abou Diaby and Eduardo Silva were injured in aggressive tackles, which – perhaps in association with a weakness in a joint – handicapped them for a long time afterwards.

This does not mean that we should have waited until the players were older before selecting them. Lionel Messi, Cristiano Ronaldo and Cesc Fàbregas all began their careers when young and did not receive injuries of that magnitude. It is a risk, but I think that players are better protected today, and in less danger than they were in those days not so long ago.

During that whole period of extremely intensive work, while also coping with the pressure from the media and fans who were demanding the same results as before without necessarily seeing what we were achieving so magnificently, heads held high, I had to deal with another change that had a huge effect on me: the departure of my great friend David Dein. It had been David who'd hired me, and he and I had worked together so incredibly well. We respected each other's complementary roles and had developed a unique relationship. By wanting to bring Stan Kroenke, a director of Arsenal since 2008 and the majority shareholder, on to the board, David had put himself in open conflict with the directors. David is an innovator, a highly sociable man with incredible tenacity and unparalleled generosity. When he left, he sold his shares to the Russian oligarch Alisher Usmanov.

With David Dein's departure, I sensed the club would change, that the Arsenal spirit would endure, but with the evolution that was occurring in football and in club ownership, even if my life as a coach stayed the same, my life as a manager would be quite different. Obviously, David and I went on seeing a lot of each other. He may have stepped away from the club but he did not distance himself from football. He often had dinner with former players, he attended matches, he continued to serve the sport with all his passion. He created an association and is involved in schools and prisons. He was the driving force behind an extraordinary initiative in which players, coaches and staff members from Premier League clubs hold twice-weekly teaching sessions in prisons, and the programme has now expanded to include around 107 prisons in England.

When I arrived, the Hill-Wood family owned the club, and had passed it down from father to son. Peter Hill-Wood was not the majority shareholder. Two other families were shareholders of the club: Danny Fiszman, who had joined the board of directors in 1992, and the Carr family. Then there were all the supporters who held one or two shares, and used to talk to me about the club as if it were their home or their family whenever I bumped into them in the street. When I arrived, a share was worth £800; it subsequently rose continuously in value and by the time I left it stood at £17,000. The value went up even more as the club's profits grew and the accumulated debt from the construction of the new stadium was reduced. I had fought hard to achieve this healthy financial situation and we succeeded.

This was the point at which the club owned by English families opened up its capital to overseas investors in a big way. The American entrepreneur Stan Kroenke would gradually become the main shareholder of the club, buying Danny Fiszman's shares. In 2010, Fiszman announced to the board that he was resigning due to ill-health. The rivalry between Usmanov, Kroenke and the traditional English shareholders would be intense. Over the years, the American would emerge the winner, with Usmanov selling him his stake in 2018, leaving Kroenke in control of 97

210

per cent of Arsenal's shares. It was also during this period that Arsenal hired Ivan Gazidis to organise the club's future structure.

At the end of the 2006–07 season, I went on holiday to Italy with my family, but I was exhausted and lacking in drive. I felt caught between my loyalty to the club, to everything that we needed to carry on doing, and my friendship with David, who has always been a staunch support for me. We had been through so many trials and tribulations, had so many adventures together: he was instrumental in recruiting me and had been a steadying influence when I first arrived; he'd been there for all our victories and when we took the decision to leave Highbury and build the new stadium.

That holiday is still a painful memory for me. I was exhausted, and wondering where all this relentless work was leading. David asked me to stay, to think only of the good of the club, but that was not enough to calm me down. I suffered a burnout. And it was Yann Rougier who helped me get back on my feet. I was like a samurai who had given his all to his passion. And I did give everything: even when I was feeling bad, I didn't do that by halves either. I very rarely did anything in moderation. I had learnt to protect myself by staying in control when inside the storm was raging. And the storm surfaced that summer.

When I returned to Arsenal, this physical and

psychological exhaustion was behind me. I quickly recovered and I did not lose my passion – quite the reverse, in fact. But I was more aware that it came at a cost to myself and others, a cost I wanted and accepted but which did not stop me from floundering and doubting.

During those years of fluctuation at the top of the club, involving many differences of opinion and rivalries, I tried to stay out of the way, concentrating each day on the next match and on the importance of building and rebuilding the team.

Arsenal at the time were mirroring what was happening around the world: the structure of football was evolving, and we were part of that. Bit by bit, clubs were being purchased by foreign buyers and the Premier League no longer belonged to the English. In 1996, I was the club's first foreign manager, and we all remember the reactions that provoked. Today, the majority of the managers are foreign, as are the owners. Only the crowd, the supporters, have not changed. We have moved gradually from supporter-owners to investor-owners, with the new rules that has imposed: all clubs have become corporate entities. The human aspect has been lost or is at least diminished. Organisations are more top heavy, and the technical side – the team, the players, the academy – is becoming smaller within companies where the commercial, marketing and press departments take up ever more space. When I started, the club had 70–80 staff; then we went to 200, 400, up to 700 staff when I left Arsenal in 2018. In the academy alone there were over 200 staff.

When a club, an organisation gets too big, there is a risk it might lose its performance culture, and instead think more about protecting personal interests and preserving the status quo. As a result, this does not allow any real innovation or genuine risk-taking.

The time available to dedicate to pure technique was reduced. I became more frustrated; it was as if I were being prevented from doing my work while I was doing it. The players and I were increasingly in demand, even though I always tried to keep some moments of solitude for myself every day and block off closed areas where the team could meet among themselves. It was no longer just a case of who you were, but the image you wanted to promote, which inevitably had repercussions on the life of a club and of a player. David Beckham was one of the first to become a media icon; the clubs followed and each has promoted itself in its own way.

When investors buy a club, they want it to work well and be profitable, and obviously their priorities are not the same as those of a supporter-owner who tends to manage a club more like a family business.

At the same time, football in general is taking a more commercial turn: domestic companies are becoming global companies, the global image of football as a business has taken precedence over its interest as a sport, the United States and China have started becoming hugely influential and, most of all, television earnings have rocketed and changed everything drastically. In 2019, Arsenal's earnings from television amounted to £180 million. Repayments for the stadium currently stand at £15 million a year: that shows just how insignificant those payments have now become.

Domestic television rights have reached a peak, and now the international rights have started to shoot up. Asia and the United States have bought the rights to the Premiership. We also had to travel the world and manage our image abroad. I have given speeches at a Beijing university to lecture halls full of students in Arsenal colours who knew the history and life of the club better than I did, and could even tell me which brand of tea I prefer. Only one or two of them had been to the Emirates themselves, but they were fervent supporters.

When you have managed a structure of this kind, when you are in charge of so many things, you feel you're always running to keep up and you're very dissatisfied. With the creation of the Human Resources department, everything becomes more bureaucratic, and of course for a manager like me who hired his first player in a motorway car park in Orange, who makes on-the-spot, instinctive decisions, this does not always suit. Another example that shows how much the job has changed: the world of transfers. Today everything is very organised, with colossal sums at stake and very precise rules. But in the past, contracts could be agreed in a more improvised way. David Dein and I were in charge of the contracts. And we sometimes found ourselves dealing with farcical situations.

I had bought Sylvinho from the Brazilian club Corinthians in 1999. And then in 2000, to replace Emmanuel Petit, I wanted to bring in Edu from the same club. One day Sylvinho called me: 'Edu is in prison!' He had been stopped on arrival at Heathrow Airport unwittingly with a counterfeit Portuguese passport, and had been immediately sent back to Brazil. We renegotiated his contract, he got some genuine documents done and was finally able to come to Arsenal in 2001. As Sylvinho had got through the same passport control as Edu, his passport must have been genuine. But deep down I always had a slight doubt. So whenever we went through passport control in airports, I made sure he was next to me. He always got through without a problem. At the end of the season, we sold Sylvinho to the Spanish club Celta Vigo and he then continued his career at Barcelona.

Being a manager really was about doing everything in all sorts of situations.

After David's departure, we became a team of three: me, Ivan Gazidis and Dick Law, who was brought in to assist me. Dick Law was very important to me. We lived through the transformation of the transfer market together. Then, thanks to the financial fair play regulations that were implemented in 2010, preventing clubs from spending money they didn't have, we were more able to compete on a level playing field with the other clubs.

During all those years, I was vigilant about one particular thing: on the technical side, the part closest to my heart, I made sure the Arsenal spirit remained unchanged. For years, we found ourselves up against very strong teams with incredible players. It was a constant battle and juggling act: we had to train the next generation of players while we fought to the death every year. And that is something that I will always love doing. It was during those years, too, that we saw how important it was to maintain the club spirit in the face of all the changes, and how important to train a very young generation of new players. Those players had some great qualities but some did not have the mental strength required to play at Arsenal. The club was carrying them rather than the other way around. When they left, many of them disappeared from circulation at the top level of the sport. One of the things we did to consolidate our values and reinforce the group feeling was to work together before the start of each season to put in place a kind of written constitution. We divided the players into groups of five and got them to write down what they thought was important about how they played and how they behaved.

We were well aware that an individual's relationship with time, the future, courtesy and respect can vary according to his education and culture. By writing this constitution with the whole club every season, we created an idea of our shared values, the ones that were most common to everyone, we clarified what we expected of each person and we became more united.

That was how I coached the players who were being lined up to take over from the magnificent Invincibles generation. Alongside the experience of William Gallas in defence, and Alexander Hleb and Tomáš Rosický in midfield, we had some extraordinary young players like Robin van Persie, Cesc Fàbregas, Samir Nasri, Emmanuel Eboué, Alex Song and Laurent Koscielny. I bought Laurent from FC Lorient in 2010. He went on to have a great career at the club, and won more than fifty caps for the French national team.

As for Fàbregas, he was vision personified, the man who saw everything before the ball reached his feet. He had a great feel for passing, long and short, and how to play with other people. He was a cut above the rest. He had a lot of personality and intelligence too. He was always hugely dissatisfied with himself, and this led to him putting himself down, even when he had been very good. He remembered only the things he had done badly, but that is often the mark of great players, and the price to pay for being great.

These players developed some interesting ideas, and often

showed the same quality of play as their predecessors, and some real talent, but we also had very worthy opponents and we lacked maturity in decisive situations. Throughout those years with no title, when Chelsea, Manchester City and Manchester United were stronger, we always found a place for ourselves thanks to these players, and we were always in the top four in what was a very difficult league. With hindsight, I know it is the Invincibles who will be remembered, yet, from my point of view, what those players who came after achieved was just as difficult. We were in the top four, we qualified for the Champions League, we progressed past the group stage, we balanced the budget. Those years were fascinating and intense. We were not as solid or effective in defence as before, but we played with style and even our opponents recognised this. It was a real treat for me to work with those players. So when I sensed they wanted to leave because they wanted trophies that they could not win with us, it was painful: even harder than with Henry, Vieira and Pirès, players who left when they were in their thirties after having given their all for us. We were now entering a period when players were leaving between 22 and 25 years old. It was as if we were being cut down before the harvest. But the salaries being offered by our competitors were huge and we couldn't compete. In 2011, the departure of two of our key players left a big gap in our team. Nasri went to Manchester City. And Fàbregas, who was then team captain, left for his home town of

Barcelona. It was hard to let players in whom we'd invested so much time and energy go.

The following year, 2012, it was Van Persie who left, for Manchester United. I had bought him in 2004 from Feyenoord where he had been playing in the reserves. He needed to progress, to toughen up. A friend in the Netherlands had recommended him to me, as had Damien Comolli who had been the under-16s coach at AS Monaco in 1992 and became our scout at Arsenal from 1998 to 2004. I got Van Persie to do some technical tests but the results were not extraordinary. More than anything, he failed a stamina test. I talked to him and during the discussion he showed such passion for the game, such shrewd analysis, such a capacity to identify his strengths and weaknesses that I decided to take him. At first he was a bit arrogant, a bit of a show-off when he played, and there was a lot of friction. That was exactly what I did not want for the team. He had a difficult relationship with Thierry Henry, and they had such different personalities. At training sessions, I encouraged him to simplify his game. He already had an amazing touch on the ball and he progressed in leaps and bounds. He was a thoroughbred player, an artist. He had such incredible class, and for me he is still a bit under-estimated as a player. In 2011, in the fifth round of the Champions League, against Barça, he was very unfairly sent off by the referee for having attempted to score after he had been whistled for offside. That affected us all. When he was dismissed, the score was 1-1. Barça won 3-1.

I had put Van Persie in as centre-forward with Fàbregas and Nasri and he'd played some outstanding matches, of unbelievable technical quality. Frequently in those years he was one of the top goalscorers in the Premier League, wearing the number 10 shirt that had once belonged to Dennis Bergkamp. And in 2011–12, he achieved the feat of scoring 30 goals in 36 league matches, equalling Thierry Henry's tally from eight years previously.

In 2012, he announced his intention not to extend his contract. All the big clubs were courting him. I sold him to Manchester United. The supporters were angry with me for this but we could not match the offer. I managed to negotiate his departure for £24 million, which was a huge amount at the time for a player with a year left on his contract. I had only the interests of the club in mind. My relationship with Alex Ferguson and Manchester United had improved by then, but every transfer is a polite game of poker where you attempt not to give anything away. Van Persie had a fantastic first six months at Old Trafford: he put the team on track for the Premiership title and made it even more difficult for us. But after three years of the four that he signed for, he was injured and Louis van Gaal sold him to the Turkish club Fenerbahçe. He called me because he wanted to come back, but it was impossible: he was at the end of his career and we were investing in young players.

Alex Song left us the same year as Van Persie, for Barça:

he also wanted to go, he had lost his appetite for playing with us.

But, for me, these players will always be Arsenal players, men who were able to play the kind of football they wanted, men who had their best years of football together.

When the financial disparity between clubs is too great, players who are going through a good patch have a tendency to dream about a big contract elsewhere and consequently tend to put their own interests first or be less committed to their club.

During those years when we didn't win the league championship, victory eluded us for some tiny thing, a weakness, a minor lapse of attention, a lack of maturity, sometimes a bit of selfishness, but we stayed in the battle with the best. We had to be constantly thinking about bringing new players into the team, players who would be a breath of fresh air while retaining the club's spirit, its uniqueness, its art. We hired.

Olivier Giroud arrived at Arsenal in 2012. He came to us from Montpellier where his results were so good that he was the best goalscorer in Ligue 1. He was 26 years old and the previous year he had also made his debut in the French national team. He commands huge respect as someone you can always rely on in adversity. When we come to look back, it will become clear that he had a great career. Through his strength and hard work he achieved

221

the recognition he deserved, both in England and France. Deep down, he has unshakeable psychological strength, the conviction that he is going to do things right and that he is going to succeed. And he is ready to prove it and pay the price for it with effort and work. Today he is the third-highest French goalscorer in Premier League history behind Thierry Henry and Nicolas Anelka: he has scored 86 goals in the Premier League. I am proud to have believed in him and to have brought all three of these strikers to England and helped them reach the summits of their capability.

Another key player joined us in 2012: Santi Cazorla. I brought him in from Málaga after two months of negotiation. He was a sensational player. He arrived with a huge smile, was always happy whenever he had the ball, and he had an incredible technique that served the team really well. I had spotted Santi thanks to my Spanish scout Francis Cagigao, and to Pirès, with whom Santi had played at Villarreal. I had seen him play and realised just how much the game was in his blood. Nobody could beat him in technical battles. He was right-footed, but he was remarkable with both feet. He considerably raised the technical level of the team in midfield.

From 2013, our heads were above water, financially. That was the moment when we made one of our most iconic transfers: Mesut Özil. It was our biggest signing for years. I had spotted the young player when he was with Werder

Bremen and I had almost recruited him before Real did. He chose the Spanish club on that occasion and stayed there for three years. I loved his playing style. He came to us from a Spanish league that was more technical but not as physically rough as the English league. That required him to adapt. He fitted easily into the team, he had great technical flair, he was in a setting that suited him and he was happy. In 2013, with him in the team, we started the season well; we were at the top of the league for several weeks. It was a mixed season for Özil: journalists and supporters were waiting to trip him up, we finished fourth in the Premiership, we qualified for the Champions League and we won the FA Cup in 2014, a long-awaited trophy that ended the season in wonderful style at Wembley.

Özil is an artist who feels football through all the pores of his skin and his soul. He needs to be constantly encouraged and he needs to feel close to his coach and have a relationship of trust with him. Being hard on him doesn't work. Like all artists, he needs to feel supported in his creativity. He has a feel for passing and an exceptional sense of timing when he passes. There is something magical and simple about his playing style. The Premier League is a train that goes by at 200 kilometres per hour, and Özil doesn't always go at this speed, but you always have great affection for his artistry.

In 2014, we were looking to get Luís Suárez over. We had an agreement with the player and his agent. But the agent claimed that there was a clause: with an offer above £40 million, Liverpool would be obliged to let the player go. But thanks to an indiscretion within Liverpool, I found out that this clause never existed. To check this was true, we offered £40,000,001. This may have seemed ludicrous, I admit. But Liverpool did not want to sell Suárez, they could afford to keep him and there was already an offer from Barça on the horizon.

In 2014, 2015 and 2017 we won the FA Cup three times and in 2016 we lost the league, coming second behind Leicester, which was seen as a failure but it has to be said that Leicester City lost only three matches in the whole season, two of which were against Arsenal. Unfortunately, we had lost Cazorla in September and this had had an impact on our technical foundations.

In those years when we had to fight hard to achieve our goals and train players, the administrative and commercial departments inside the club were growing. The technical and scientific staff around the team was also expanding. We had to fight to retain clarity in the organisation and protect the unique club spirit.

I consider transfers to be an integral part of a manager's work, and the season's success depends in large part on the quality of the work done during the transfer windows. However, I am in favour of removing the mid-season transfer window, because it destabilises the players during the season and every setback then becomes an opportunity for them to ask themselves if they wouldn't be better off elsewhere.

As I said before, negotiation is a difficult art that requires some of the skills of a poker player.

Every transfer takes place in a very emotional context. I remember one particular negotiation in the middle of the 1998 World Cup. We had a meeting with West Ham United and Ian Wright for his transfer. We didn't yet know that Aimé Jacquet and Zinedine Zidane would take France to footballing heaven. Seated around a table on a sunny restaurant terrace were Ian Wright, the directors of West Ham, David Dein, his daughter Sasha and me. After the usual niceties, we began negotiating. Sasha, staying discreetly in the background, was a huge fan of Ian Wright, and she gradually realised that we were selling her idol, her favourite player. Without uttering a word, she carried on eating but tears were flowing silently onto her plate. That symbolises exactly what transfers mean to supporters: sometimes intense pain, but at other times, incredible happiness and hope.

In the world of football, and especially during the transfer window, being easy prey encourages others to eat you alive.

During my time at Arsenal, I was involved in 450 transfers. I was always guided by the wish to strike a deal in the most straightforward, uncomplicated way possible.

Looking back, that was a good thing: in twenty-two years there were no legal problems.

I recruited some players after seeing them play on television. Others I already knew, such as Patrick Vieira, Thierry Henry and Emmanuel Petit. And some were brought to my attention by my recruiters and scouts. When you buy players, you don't always have the opportunity to check them out first, even when the players are very young. You trust the recruiters, especially when the players are very young. I did not see Cesc Fàbregas play before my recruiter strongly recommended that we acquired him.

Some transfers, of course, are regrettable. Serge Gnabry, an all-round attacker with a very promising future, made his debut for Arsenal at the age of seventeen and after a serious knee injury, a loan spell at West Bromwich Albion and a transfer to Werder Bremen, he ended up as a Bayern Munich Player of the Season.

I recruited the South Korean striker Park Chu-young because he had enjoyed a great season with Monaco and had a very good attitude. I don't think he was able to fully express his game with us. I am not questioning his talent. No doubt he lacked a bit of self-confidence. He never found the game that changed everything, the game where he could tell himself: 'Hey, I'm actually good enough to play here.' Perhaps I didn't give him enough chances to prove himself.

I have been asked why the German international Lukas

Podolski, a prolific scorer for the national team, did not play frequently enough, and why he tended to be deployed on the left wing rather than through the centre, but I don't believe he played more or fewer times than many of the others. I put him on when I thought it was a good time to use him.

Those transfers, when we were selling our players as well as buying from other clubs, always led to huge debates about money: the club's money, the money spent on a player, and on players' and coaches' salaries, how a particular manager has a reputation for being a spendthrift or, conversely, very careful with his budget. Money is always a core issue. I was often asked about our players' salaries: up to what point is a salary reasonable? I have always answered in the same way: a salary is reasonable as long as it does not destabilise a club's budget. I nonetheless understand that in some respects these salaries can shock people. That is why I think that clubs should be wholly private and not receive any public subsidies. Salaries are only justifiable in football if the income equals the expenditure. The wealth of football nowadays comes from television earnings. Between my arrival at Arsenal in 1996 and my departure from the club in 2018, TV income increased eight-fold. This explains the increase in salaries, and everything points to the fact that the rise is only going to continue.

I have probably got my own particular relationship to money due to my personality and my past history. I started out with nothing, on a shoestring, travelling around on my own to purchase and negotiate the price of individual footballs, one by one, sleeping in lumpy beds the night before matches, travelling with my team in second-class couchettes on overnight trains. Later I came to be awash with footballs, I've stayed in marvellous hotels and travelled in private jets. The scenery has changed but deep down, what really makes the night or the journey comfortable is winning the match.

If money had been my priority instead of passion or loyalty, I could have earned two or three times more by leaving Arsenal and moving from one club to another. I have always thought first and foremost of my responsibilities and the future of my club; I did not want anyone to be able to say that I had managed things badly. I wanted balance above all. Today Arsenal is in a strong and healthy financial position. We repaid our loans without external support, by selling our best players for a good price and by being careful. The press and the supporters sometimes criticised me for my transfers but I paid off our debt. We have always sold very well. And that is how I built my reputation on the transfer market: thanks to intuition, experience, my scouts who were looking for players that suited us, and thanks to the situation of the club and my character that obliged us to be fair and firm. We were already thinking in terms of financial fair play even before those rules were implemented, and we actively fought for it. Our only way of competing on equal terms with other clubs was for them to stop investing money they didn't have. Once financial fair play came in, it made competition between clubs fairer and healthier, but today I would fight for less strict rules on investment in football and better monitoring of club management. Relaxing the rules of financial fair play would be welcome so that clubs could evolve, not get stuck in a situation where you have some very good, very powerful clubs and others that are restricted because they lack the ability to invest. If this does not happen, there's no way to change the balance of power. Transforming a club takes time and money. Those who have a strong position in the hierarchy today are where they are because they invested when financial fair play did not exist.

And whenever we think about transfers and the issue of money in football, we immediately think of agents. When I started playing, there was no such thing as players' and managers' agents. I have always represented myself because that suited my personality, my desire to be free, and I have never had an agent. Nowadays, everybody has one. I have had a financial adviser, Léon Angel, who has been with me from the start, and a commercial and image consultant, Serge Kotchounian. Over the years, Serge has become much more than this, and he is a man I trust completely. But I have always wanted to negotiate my job contracts on my own. Television was an entirely different world, and Serge has always been and still is invaluable in helping me make choices and feel free. We met in Monaco and became very close. He travels with me everywhere.

Agents are there to help players negotiate their contracts. It is illogical that they are paid by the clubs, not the players. But that is how it has always worked and it inevitably drives prices up, with clubs outbidding one another. When I was at Arsenal, we limited agent commissions to 5 per cent of the player's annual salary, but bit by bit the percentage has increased. It went up to 7 or 8 per cent and now clubs pay 10 per cent. Agents and players alike are becoming wealthier and more powerful. As in any other profession, every agent has a different approach: there are very good ones who give good advice, who are an invaluable support for the player, there are those who think only of their own interests and there are those who are dangerous to the point of threatening their players. It is a murky, ever-changing, diverse profession that evolves as football evolves. There are those who make a very good living and others who depend on one player and are in a weak position because everyone knows just how transient it all is. They can be fired from one day to the next due to a difference of opinion, a family member who wants to take their place or a stronger agent seeking to benefit from the work they have already done. It is a difficult and thankless task, and for managers, the art of transfers, and of the market, consists of being wary, being firm, weighing up the influence that money has on the player and trying as far as possible to deal only with people who know the world of top-level football well, who understand the high demands, who have a strong analytical capacity. An agent must be capable of spotting a talented player, supporting him in the best way possible while being aware of the difficult, unrewarding, monotonous lives that top sportspeople lead, lives ruled by performance and repetitive daily rituals. Alas, I find that the world of football is populated by men with only a superficial knowledge of the game and top-level sport. Fake specialists with fixed opinions who are prepared to lie to their players in order to keep them. As a coach, I have often had to do battle with agents who were telling their players things that were the complete opposite of what I felt to be right, for example, in situations where I spotted something missing, something wrong, fatigue, apathy. And because of this, I occasionally had to take the drastic decision to part with a player. Because the dialogue, our work together, could no longer be real, we were not understanding each other as we should have been.

Talking to agents, getting to know them, meeting them frequently throughout the negotiation period, and then throughout the duration of their players' contracts, is an integral part of a manager's schedule. And a very good agent assists the coach and the manager in their work. As a manager, I established a certain distance between the player and myself; I did not get involved in his private life, when or where he went out or his personal relationships, his wife, except if the player asked me for advice or wanted me to get involved. This only happened on rare occasions. The manager is there for the game, for the sport. An agent does not have that distance. He is much more involved, hence his crucial role and his influence. Which is why I always told young players to surround themselves with good people. A 23-year-old player who hasn't been careful about choosing those around him, who hasn't identified the bad influences, any jealousies, people who are a handicap to his career, a relative who is overly present, an adviser who is not a specialist, is, as I see it, in a difficult position that is unsustainable at the top level. As someone who has never had an agent but who has seen that all managers have one nowadays, I've always thought that the same rule that applies to players should also apply to managers: you need good people around you.

A manager must have his own entourage. A manager lives in a totally unsettled world, where results are precarious and his perceived value fluctuates from one day to the next. It is hard to stand tall and stay firm about your principles when things are not going as you want. This is why it is vital to create an active structure around you, men who are united and stand together. I had Pat Rice, Boro, Gary Lewin's physio team, Steve Bould, Tony Colbert, Gerry Peyton, Sean O'Connor, Steve Braddock, Steve Rowley – all remarkable men. As a player, Steve

Bould had great commitment in defence, and achieved an excellent technical level, and he has a very good knowledge of the game. He was also highly appreciated as a coach.

I also had some fine doctors who helped me throughout my career: Crane, Beasley, O'Driscoll. Whenever I arrived at a club, I always tried to surround myself straight away with competent people who knew the club and the culture. Today, it's a bit different: managers – like players – come with their own structure, ready-made teams who leave with them, a group that works like a club within a club. I never wanted that. That is part of how the job is evolving. Both the manager and his entourage must work for the club, and I was lucky to be involved in a long-term process that allowed me to build and progress little by little with men I trusted totally.

However, I always knew that I was ultimately the one in charge: it's the manager alone who decides; he takes advice from everyone else but it is his final decision that counts and it is he who is resented for it. Before every match, he makes some people unhappy, players who are not playing and feel disappointed, betrayed or sad. They might complain, disconnect from the group spirit, and that can destroy the team's energy. Managing means taking action and making decisions, while accepting a degree of uncertainty. One must constantly repair strained relationships, with players, agents and supporters. And during difficult moments for the club, it can be tough, but that's how it is: you turn more to your assistants, to the club, than to your friends and loved ones.

In 2014, we managed to sign Alexis Sánchez. We came to an agreement with his agent and Barça after the player had had a superb season at the Spanish club, which finished second in the Spanish league that year, scoring 19 goals. He was explosive, unpredictable and incredibly hungry. He was a centre-forward but he moved around the field and brought great energy to the team. He was a wild footballer with extraordinary determination, the kind of personality that sometimes made him a bit different from the rest of the team and which meant he was spirited and uncompromising. He had an all-or-nothing, surly personality, his own very individual style.

Three years later, with Sánchez well established in the side, in the round of 16 against Bayern Munich we lost badly at the Emirates while playing with ten men. I had no way of knowing it was to be my last Champions League match as the manager of Arsenal.

However, in 2017, we beat top-of-the-league Chelsea in the FA Cup final 2-1 with an Aaron Ramsey winning goal again, after having beaten Manchester City in the semis. For the first time in twenty-one years, we finished outside the top four in the Premiership, on 75 points.

*

Things were getting more and more difficult at Arsenal. The supporters were impatient, the public was turning against me and I had the impression that the general atmosphere was just like the one that had greeted me when I first arrived at the club. I know twenty-two years leading a club is wonderful, but I wasn't ready to go; if it had just been up to me I would have stayed until my contract expired. I told myself I had given a lot, sacrificed a lot for the club, and I felt that the hostility of a section of the fans and the board was unjustified. I felt as if I'd built the training centre and the stadium myself brick by brick, and that my car drove there every morning of its own accord. Not being able to go there from one day to the next, no longer going to the matches, no longer living my passion for the club, was very hard, very brutal. Arsenal was a matter of life and death to me, and without it there were some very lonely, very painful moments.

I had managed Arsenal for 1,235 official matches, and my last match at the Emirates on 6 May 2018 is a particularly poignant memory. We were playing against Burnley and we won 5-0. We had put on a display that of course I was happy about, but all of a sudden, watching the match, the farewell ceremony, looking at the stands, I remembered everything we had gone through together, the stadium that had cost us so much, that we had put all our strength into building. I contained my emotion as best I could, I invited some friends to dinner and tried to convince myself that life would go on.

After some days of sadness, I succeeded. The handover was difficult. I deliberately kept out of the way, I had to keep my head down, even though it seemed to me that the people making the decisions for the club knew it less well than I did.

We know that in football there are times when teams are stronger and times when they are weaker. People all over the world have loved this club because it was more than just a team: it embodied a way of making the sport live, with passion, fairness and class. Our values showed in our results, of course, but also in the way we were, the way we behaved, the way we spoke at all times. Every club has a culture that can be momentarily forgotten but it always resurfaces. Mikel Arteta took charge of the team in December 2019, and with him these values, this spirit, this style that was characteristic of the club can once again come to the fore. As an Arsenal player, he was passionate, intelligent, and had the ardour and determination of youth, and he has not lost that, I believe. For me, he was an invaluable go-between with the team. He has the experience, the desire that is needed to revive the soul of the club, and made a great start with an FA Cup final win over Chelsea in his first season in charge. On the whole, I think it is down to former players like Pirès, Vieira and Henry to take on positions of power in football.

One should never relive old love affairs: Arsenal is a fundamental part of my life, my heart, my memories, but it is not for me to think about its future, to guide it. A new generation is coming up, it is their challenge to take on.

FIFA has offered me another.

When I look back, I realise I have been enormously lucky in life. I have worked with the best, met the best people in sport and industry. The common denominator for any success is a combination of attitude, talent and external luck. People at the top are also capable of objectively analysing their own performance and are hard on themselves. A good balance between intelligence and constant motivation and a good dose of humility. Humility in sport is knowing that past performance gives you credibility but does not confer any privileges. Humility is the only thing that enables you to maintain the degree of vigilance that is essential for remaining steadfast.

I am also aware that for now I am leaving a profession that is constantly evolving. Today's manager uses persuasion. The action he needs to take should be based on a three-pronged approach: *giving people responsibilities, personalising,* and *openness*, through clear and constant communication, based on today's science for preparing and analysing his job. The coach must not forget that in order to take others with him, towards the values that he advocates, he must embody these values himself.

It is also essential that the player remembers that talent can go to waste if it is not accompanied by effort. Having a kind of dissatisfaction within oneself, which is often a kind of tension, enables people to move up to the next level. In my experience, working on all the areas necessary and putting in the sustained effort that's required is something you will see in only the very best.

'I often imagine the first words I will exchange with God when I die. He will ask me what I did with my life, what meaning I gave it. I'll tell him I tried to win matches! "That's all?'" he'll probably ask, disappointed. I'll try to convince him that winning matches is harder than you might think, and that football is important to millions of people's lives, that it creates moments for sharing, moments of joy, and great sadness too.'

10

MY LIFE AFTER ARSENAL

My departure from Arsenal was a very tough, very painful moment.

For as long as I could remember I had lived in football and for football.

Football determined the pace of my whole life. At night, when I got home after a long day at the club, I'd watch more matches that would throw me back into the work I was planning to do the following day with the team – how I was going to settle certain problems, how I was going to keep making progress. When I went to bed, I would be thinking over my day, and the next: the players, the matches and the training sessions populated my nights.

It was a real vocation, a monastic life devoted to football, a life chosen with passion, perhaps also sometimes with a bit of madness and some sacrifices.

I often imagine the first words I will exchange with God when I die. He will ask me what I did with my life, what meaning I gave it. I'll tell him I tried to win matches! 'That's all?' he'll probably ask, disappointed. I'll try to convince him that winning matches is harder than you might think, and that football is important to millions of people's lives, that it creates moments for sharing, moments of joy, and great sadness too.

I had to learn to live without Arsenal, without that constant tension, without the players I loved, without that pitch, that turf that was my adrenaline, my drug, my reason for living. But I cannot give up my passion, I can't give up the adventure. Ever since my childhood, I've always wanted a life made up of adventures and people, of risks. Even today. I'm 70 years old and I don't know what tomorrow will bring. I divide my time between London, Paris and Zurich, I move around a lot, I'm often living in hotels.

I have received and I continue to receive countless proposals that would bring me back to competitive football, back onto the pitch, back into the action. And I'm always touched to bump into supporters who ask me what my next club is going to be, trying to predict where I might go.

*

It was David Dein who first talked to me about FIFA and urged me to consider their offer. He knew how sad I'd been since leaving Arsenal. Ever since my departure, in May 2018, we had met up every week to discuss the club and its future. We were always talking about this club we had so loved, for which we had done so much. What would become of it?

We were both facing the same difficulty: not being able to act. It's a hard position to accept for men who have spent their lives making decisions, getting things done. But you need to know how to step aside, to accept it with dignity and with respect for those who come after you.

David was less radical than me. He still goes to watch matches at the Emirates. I watch them on television. The stadium I built and whose every little secret I know is somewhere I can no longer go: it's still too emotional. Likewise the training centre that was my favourite place, in the middle of the countryside.

I keep myself away from the club but that doesn't prevent me, like all the other fans, from continuing to follow it passionately, and to wonder where it's headed. I had given myself to it completely, my heart, my head and my body, and even if I'm no longer the manager, my heart still belongs to the club. If you love Arsenal once, you love it for ever.

I still have friends there, of course, who sometimes keep me up to speed, who tell me about their lives and the life of the club, but when you leave, you have to really leave. You shouldn't let things get blurry. That's not good for you or for the club. You are either inside or outside. Today, after some difficult months, I have accepted that it is over and I await the new generation of coaches, the generation of former players who will take the club's destiny in hand and restore the spirit they used to know.

When he spoke to me about FIFA, David said, 'It's time for you to serve football now.' He invited me to act more globally, to think about football differently, to take action to benefit football, to put my experience, my competence, the knowledge I had accumulated over the years to the service of football in general, and no longer to a club as I had always done before.

Keeping this in mind, and considering everything that was at stake and the countless challenges that need to be dealt with to develop football and to promote it globally, on 13 November 2019 I took up my post as FIFA's head of Global Football Development.

Before accepting this new post, I thought about what I had to offer, about what was essential to me and how FIFA could act to put forward reforms, to think about the football of tomorrow and to shake up some of the entrenched mindsets. I had ideas about refereeing, about the coaching that is at the heart of what I know, about management, about training and development.

FIFA has incredible power but it is a gigantic organisation, with 211 national associations, which means things can be cumbersome when it comes to taking decisions and action. I needed to be sure I would be able to act effectively by creating a structure on a human scale, with professionals I could manage very autonomously.

From now on, this is the mission that occupies my thoughts.

FIFA has three main roles: *organising competitions, enacting the laws of football globally,* and *education and pedagogy.*

I see my role as contributing to the effectiveness of its educational and pedagogical mission. I have a clear vision about what needs to be done, and since arriving I have shared it with my team.

I would like to create a research centre in Zurich, for the development of football teaching methods, the laws of football and the development of technological metrics in all countries. This research centre would benefit all the associations.

I would also like to focus on the development of young players and ensure that every child has the same opportunities for success, whether they are in Europe or in Africa. That is not the case today. We also need more competitions. It is an important task, which is why we are thinking today about using new teaching methods, including in particular an online programme, with training sessions according to age group and the means to measure the effectiveness of these training sessions.

We should also take a proper interest in women's football, which has attracted the attention of the general public since the World Cup that was held in France. At Arsenal we had a women's team that was among the best. England was ahead of France in women's football, with more teams and more money, as well as greater interest.

During the World Cup we learnt how enjoyable and how interesting this football was to watch, and that the playing style tended to emphasise the collective aspect of the game, with great intelligence. It's a less physical game than the men's, certainly, but just as full of passion. There is less brutality, fewer cards, fewer interruptions and therefore more play.

I think the great challenge of women's football in the coming years is a technical one: the money and the media interest will come afterwards. The players need to gain in technical precision, but with specific training, and by developing their existing playing style, that precision will come, because there's a fierce desire to put on a display of beautiful football, to train and to make progress.

Then there is the issue of soccer in the US. At the beginning of my career, I was not really aware of soccer in the US. There had been an attempt to develop the game in the 1970s with the New York Cosmos, an elitist attempt that

ARSENAL'S KIT BY SEASON

THE EVOLUTION OF ARSENAL SHIRTS DURING ARSÈNE WENGER'S REIGN

Images reproduced by kind permission of the Premier League

1996/97

HOME KIT   AWAY KIT

1997/98

HOME KIT   AWAY KIT

1998/99

HOME KIT

AWAY KIT

1999/00

HOME KIT

AWAY KIT

2000/1

HOME KIT

AWAY KIT

2001/2

HOME KIT   AWAY KIT

2002/3

HOME KIT   AWAY KIT

2003/4

HOME KIT   AWAY KIT

2004/5

HOME KIT   AWAY KIT

2005/6

HOME KIT   AWAY KIT

2006/7

HOME KIT   AWAY KIT

2007/8

HOME KIT

AWAY KIT

2008/9

HOME KIT

AWAY KIT

2009/10

HOME KIT

AWAY KIT

2010/11

HOME KIT

AWAY KIT

2011/12

HOME KIT

AWAY KIT

2012/13

HOME KIT

AWAY KIT

2013/14

HOME KIT

AWAY KIT

2014/15

HOME KIT

AWAY KIT

THIRD KIT

2015/16

HOME KIT

AWAY KIT

THIRD KIT

2016/17

HOME KIT

AWAY KIT

THIRD KIT

2017/18

HOME KIT

AWAY KIT

THIRD KIT

*Due to digital archiving restraints, third kits before
2014-2015 are not available.

had no real fanbase or popular interest. It disappeared very quickly. Soccer got swallowed up by other American sports like basketball, baseball and American football.

The situation has changed now, and spectacularly so. Immigration to the United States has brought with it some great football enthusiasts: for example, from Central and South America and from Africa. The first football-loving immigrants were English, Irish, Scottish and Welsh, and they brought their passion for their favourite clubs along with them. It was a good foundation. But today's society is more alert to the dangers in sports, and in American football especially. Parents are more inclined to encourage their children to play soccer rather than more violent contact sports.

What's still missing, and this is a handicap, is the fact that the teaching of sport is half-yearly in the United States: a seven-year-old who plays for six months won't have the same opportunities as a European child who plays for ten or eleven months. The technical difference then becomes obvious. Football is essentially a technical sport, and the acquiring of that technique happens between the ages of seven and twelve. After this, the room for manoeuvre is very much reduced. The quality of training at that age is crucial, and America ought to focus on that. Centres of excellence are required.

What is also needed is the development of high-quality coaches. In Europe, sport develops well when the teaching of it happens not through schools but through the federations. Schools don't have sufficiently specialised coaches to teach football, whereas a federation has the means and the dedicated expertise and qualified coaches for the training. As long as sport, and learning about sport, relies entirely on schools, the sport will not be sufficiently competitive. That's one of the big challenges.

It goes without saying that the United States is a vast country. Centres of excellence must be created where the best can quickly be grouped together. It has become clear that having a high concentration of very good players is a decisive factor. What is important is the number of good players per square metre, rather than the number of good players per se. Concentration creates stimulation. It is as if you put a lot of good children in the same class rather than one good pupil isolated amid average pupils. In conversation with an accomplished table-tennis player, he told me that among the seven best players of the sport in England, four come from the same street. They play against one another and they are stimulated by the competition that provides. If we are to create an elite, the best must be brought together.

It is evident that American players, the best of them, are going to come over to play for the best European clubs. Americans have a positive attitude: they are more than ready to make every effort to get better.

Many top American soccer players have been goalkeepers.

That is perhaps the easiest position to develop at first. It is possible to create a specialised 'keepers' school', with teaching based on the repetition of individual moves, and in this way you can put together an individual training package. Whereas for the other positions in the team, you need the whole team and a more collective organisation.

I also think about the training of coaches. To train better coaches, everything happens through education, the involvement of the federation and putting the coaches into contact with top-level sport. The coaches should not be isolated, but they should go into the best clubs in order to understand the needs and demands of elite sport. We need to aim for high-quality training for coaches. The USA stages the World Cup in 2026. Six years isn't a long time! They need to hurry if they are to attain this higher level.

The global popularity of the Premier League is obvious, and it is connected to the strong English influence on the game and its very high standard. A fan today has three levels of passion. He or she might support the national team, a global top-flight team or league, and on a third level the local team. Three strata. Sometimes they become muddled. But what we notice is that the stratum at the local level is crumbling, because fans have access to the top stratum all the time and they demand greater quality at a high level. The Americans are no different. They want to watch the best, and the Premier League is a global championship.

I watch basketball a lot. There are interesting parallels

between the two sports. In the training of young footballers, basketball is an instructive sport. Speedier combinations with other players are possible. You can pass more quickly with your hands than with your feet, and so you develop better connections with other players.

As for FIFA's key role in establishing and implementing the laws of the game, it has a responsibility to ensure that these laws are applicable everywhere so as not to create two-tier football. But it is important also to preserve the spectacle that the game offers.

Each match is a story that should capture the imagination of those who are watching it, a story that remains in people's memories, so much so that some fans are still able to tell the story thirty years later with precision and so much emotion.

In the past few years, changes in the rules of refereeing have helped make football more entertaining to those watching, making the game fairer but also faster, even more interesting. These developments should be supported and extended.

I experienced all sorts of different situations as a player and as a coach when it came to referees and refereeing. For a long time the authorities were too lax with refereeing, allowing inexplicable, inexcusable mistakes to go unnoticed, so much so that players, coaches and fans felt a strong sense of injustice, some real anger.

My relations with the referees were quite distant. Maybe it was wrong of me, but I was never interested in knowing who was going to referee a particular match. In actual fact, I tended to start out with an open mind, imagining that the refereeing would be fair and impartial, but I did often find myself confronted with really flagrant refereeing mistakes.

I did sometimes lose my cool, and had tense exchanges of views with certain referees and got penalised for that. I knew I ought to stay calm, and that being too tense and too involved in the match, under too much pressure, changes our perspective, our perception. But when the mistake was too obvious and had such huge consequences, I couldn't hold back my indignation.

I got myself sent off a few times. Like in Manchester when the referee told me to go up into the stands at Old Trafford. I didn't have a seat, I was lost amid the home fans, standing there, boiling with rage. To me that wasn't entertainment: at that moment it really was a matter of life and death. At any rate, that was how I experienced it.

Today refereeing has very much been taken in hand; the people doing the job are professionals who have been through very thorough and demanding training. Referees are better trained, better selected and better monitored to ensure greater fairness in our sport. And VAR has also made it possible to guide refereeing better, to make the decisions fairer. In this regard FIFA has a huge and exciting role to play.

Among the changes to be made, one of our biggest challenges will be our ability to master the application of the technology, the precision that the technology offers, VAR in particular, more than we have been able to do thus far.

For example, the offside issue is still a problem because it requires stopping the video and examining it to the split second. During the time this checking takes, the game is stopped and the watching fans are left sidelined as the level of intensity in the stadium plummets. The anticipated improvements to VAR will make the game much more fluid.

Football should not be set in stone. It should be made to evolve towards more transparency in the game. This is essential, and that is also why I have chosen to get involved in these changes. By getting football to evolve in this way, we can restore it to what it really is: an art, a collective art.

Among my missions at FIFA, there is one that is particularly close to my heart: the training of coaches and the follow-up with former players who after their careers have ended would be keen to occupy leadership positions in clubs or on football's official bodies.

After my time as a player, although I had mentors and role models, when I became a coach I learnt as I went along. I learnt from the job, from the team, from the challenges, and I never stopped making progress. Maybe we had more time to prove ourselves. There was no structured training, and little help: the coach was alone and had to depend entirely or almost entirely on himself. Today the profession has become more organised, even though there is not yet a global coaches' union. But there is more training, and, on behalf of FIFA and other bodies, I am constantly telling people about my journey, my experience, and showing what I believe our profession is and what our responsibility is.

The means at our disposal are more numerous, especially with all the data we can use on player performance. It is all the more important that a good coach knows how to analyse these data and to use all the new technologies so they can lean on the information to follow a player's progress more fairly, more successfully. That can prevent them from 'killing' a young player, and they won't hold back his or her development, or limit their capacity to take decisions.

My responsibility today is to throw myself completely into this role at FIFA and to convey what I have learnt, especially to those youngsters who ask me: 'What is a coach? What is a manager?' Nothing can replace what they will discover for themselves, from their own experiences. But they can reflect on and be enriched by the teachings I have been able to draw out of so many years in the profession and involvement in the world of football.

For me, a coach is somebody who knows what they want, who has a clear vision, a strategy.

Who is capable of expressing it clearly.

Who puts their ideas into practice and is capable of getting their players to support their plans.

So they should be a good communicator.

A coach is somebody who can handle stress, judgement, pressure. Who remains lucid, who in difficult situations is able to take a step back, look at the situation from above. Who does not respond to stress with passivity or aggressiveness.

A coach is someone of strong convictions, who through their behaviour, values and words influences the life and style of a team as well as the life and style of a player. The coach must earn their players' respect, and their trust.

A coach is someone of experience who knows how to make themselves understood by young people, who by definition do not have their experience: listening, adapting, sometimes changing strategy, and keeping an open mind.

A coach is also a humane, compassionate person who loves their players and is able to point out their faults, their shortcomings, with a know-how that keeps their motivation and wish to excel intact.

A coach is someone who seeks out the best, who aims for excellence: for themselves first of all, getting completely involved, without letting up, not neglecting a single detail, focusing their attention on each one. And who also demands the best of their players, pushing them constantly to excel, all the while knowing that even the greatest athletes are not always performing at 100 per cent, and that they need to be pushed to surpass themselves.

Coaches ought also to be aware of the responsibility that football has, the power this sport has for young people, for society, the appeal it exercises, the fascination, sometimes the devotion it elicits. A coach, then, is someone who has a duty to be equal to this power and to make this game as beautiful as it can be, to show the art of football at its purest.

EPILOGUE

Today I still have the discipline I acquired over all those years. As I often say, freedom is in the discipline you impose on yourself. I start my day with an hour and a half in the gym, without exception, even Saturday and Sunday. When I get the chance, I'm always ready to do another hour of cardio. This iron discipline, I have to acknowledge, helps me maintain my energy levels and stay in shape, because I'm still travelling a lot and I have other activities besides my role with FIFA.

I'm a match commentator for BeIN Sports, and I'm often asked to give interviews and talks in the business world, to share my experience, the things I can teach from my life as a coach. The parallels between the sporting world and the business world are real, and arouse a great deal of interest.

But this post-Arsenal life also allows me to do things other than football, like keeping up with the news from around the world. I'm interested in everything, passionate about everything – well, almost everything – and especially economics, politics and science. I have time to read: magazines, novels, philosophy. In today's society, the relationship people have with religion, the search for happiness, for freedom, is something I find fascinating. I go to the cinema, the theatre, and I even occasionally have time to watch some TV series. I also have more time for my friends, and for my daughter with whom I can now share moments I hadn't been able to before. And that's precious to me. Having time available is of no small value, and maybe I also rate that a bit more highly at my age.

I've been very lucky in my life; it has been and still is more beautiful than anything I could have imagined as a child in my little Alsatian village. I have fulfilled my dreams, even those I must have carried within me without daring to express them. In a way, I have surpassed my wildest dreams.

I have travelled the world to experience powerful emotions and to live as fully as possible through this life of discoveries, and that total freedom to which I aspired as a boy. For me, football has always been an adventure. That is how I still experience it today.

What matters, I think, is that you retain your childlike soul and never lose sight of your dreams: what are they, what do you need technically to make them come true (abilities, means . . .); discard any negative ideas that might prevent you from getting there, and above all commit completely.

I'm sure that all lives are incomplete, but I still have so many things to do: for football, for the people I love, for myself.

I'm a lucky man, happy to be able to keep on sustaining football, developing it and sharing the joy that it brings. And I would like to help to make it more beautiful still, for all those who love it.

CAREER RECORD

with special thanks to
Steven McCann and John English

PLAYER STATISTICS

APPEARANCES AND GOALS BY CLUB, SEASON AND COMPETITION

Club	Season	League			National Cup		Europe		Total	
		Division	Apps	Goals	Apps	Goals	Apps	Goals	Apps	Goals
Mutzig	1969–70	CFA					—			
	1970–71	Division 3					—			
	1971–72	Division 3					—			
	1972–73	Division 3			3	1	—		3	1
	Total				3	1	—		3	1
FC Mulhouse	1973–74	Ligue 2	25	2			—		25	2
	1974–75	Ligue 2	31	2			—		31	2
	Total		56	4			—		56	4
ASPV Strasbourg	1975–76	Bas-Rhin			3	1	—		3	1
	1976–77	Division d'Honneur			5	0	—		5	0
	1977–78	Division 3					—			
	Total				8	1	—		8	1
RC Strasbourg	1978–79	Ligue 1	2	0			1	0	3	0
	1979–80	Ligue 1	1	0					1	0
	1980–81	Ligue 1	8	0	1	0	—		9	0
	Total		11	0	1	0	1	0	13	0
Career total			67	4	12	2	1	0	80	6

Source: Footballdatabase.eu, Racingstub.com

ARSENAL MANAGER STATISTICS

LEAGUE TABLES

1996–97

(from left to right):
Played/Wins/Draws/Losses/Goals For/Goals Against/Goal Difference/Points

1	Manchester United (C)	38	21	12	5	76	44	32	75
2	Newcastle United	38	19	11	8	73	40	33	68
3	Arsenal	38	19	11	8	62	32	30	68
4	Liverpool	38	19	11	8	62	37	25	68
5	Aston Villa	38	17	10	11	47	34	13	61
6	Chelsea	38	16	11	11	58	55	3	59
7	Sheffield Wednesday	38	14	15	9	50	51	−1	57
8	Wimbledon	38	15	11	12	49	46	3	56
9	Leicester City	38	12	11	15	46	54	−8	47
10	Tottenham Hotspur	38	13	7	18	44	51	−7	46
11	Leeds United	38	11	13	14	28	38	−10	46
12	Derby County	38	11	13	14	45	58	−13	46
13	Blackburn Rovers	38	9	15	14	42	43	−1	42
14	West Ham United	38	10	12	16	39	48	−9	42
15	Everton	38	10	12	16	44	57	−13	42
16	Southampton	38	10	11	17	50	56	−6	41
17	Coventry City	38	9	14	15	38	54	−16	41
18	Sunderland (R)	38	10	10	18	35	53	−18	40
19	Middlesbrough (R)	38	10	12	16	51	60	−9	39[d]
20	Nottingham Forest (R)	38	6	16	16	31	59	−28	34

SEASON STATS

League Position: 3rd

Managers: Stewart Houston, Arsene Wenger (first match in charge 12 October 1996)

Top Goalscorer: Ian Wright (23)

Most Assists: Dennis Bergkamp (9)

Most Appearances: Nigel Winterburn (38)

Biggest Win: ARS 4–1 SHW (H)

Heaviest Defeat: LIV 2–0 ARS (A)

1997–98

1	Arsenal (C)	38	23	9	6	68	33	35	78
2	Manchester United	38	23	8	7	73	26	47	77
3	Liverpool	38	18	11	9	68	42	26	65
4	Chelsea	38	20	3	15	71	43	28	63
5	Leeds United	38	17	8	13	57	46	11	59
6	Blackburn Rovers	38	16	10	12	57	52	5	58
7	Aston Villa	38	17	6	15	49	48	1	57
8	West Ham United	38	16	8	14	56	57	−1	56
9	Derby County	38	16	7	15	52	49	3	55
10	Leicester City	38	13	14	11	51	41	10	53

11	Coventry City	38	12	16	10	46	44	2	52
12	Southampton	38	14	6	18	50	55	−5	48
13	Newcastle United	38	11	11	16	35	44	−9	44
14	Tottenham Hotspur	38	11	11	16	44	56	−12	44
15	Wimbledon	38	10	14	14	34	46	−12	44
16	Sheffield Wednesday	38	12	8	18	52	67	−15	44
17	Everton	38	9	13	16	41	56	−15	40
18	Bolton Wanderers (R)	38	9	13	16	41	61	−20	40
19	Barnsley (R)	38	10	5	23	37	82	−45	35
20	Crystal Palace (R)	38	8	9	21	37	71	−34	33

SEASON STATS

League Position: 1st

Managers: Arsene Wenger

Top Goalscorer: Dennis Bergkamp (16)

Most Assists: Dennis Bergkamp (11)

Most Appearances: Nigel Winterburn (36)

Biggest Win: ARS 5–0 BAR (H)

Heaviest Defeat: LIV 4–0 ARS (A)

1998–99

1	Manchester United (C)	38	22	13	3	80	37	43	79
2	Arsenal	38	22	12	4	59	17	42	78
3	Chelsea	38	20	15	3	57	30	27	75
4	Leeds United	38	18	13	7	62	34	28	67
5	West Ham United	38	16	9	13	46	53	−7	57
6	Aston Villa	38	15	10	13	51	46	5	55
7	Liverpool	38	15	9	14	68	49	19	54
8	Derby County	38	13	13	12	40	45	−1	52
9	Middlesbrough	38	12	15	11	48	54	−6	51
10	Leicester City	38	12	13	13	40	46	−6	49
11	Tottenham Hotspur	38	11	14	13	47	50	−3	47
12	Sheffield Wednesday	38	13	7	18	41	42	−1	46
13	Newcastle United	38	11	13	14	48	54	−6	46
14	Everton	38	11	10	17	42	47	−5	43
15	Coventry City	38	11	9	18	39	51	−12	42
16	Wimbledon	38	10	12	16	40	63	−23	42
17	Southampton	38	11	8	19	37	64	−27	41
18	Charlton Athletic (R)	38	8	12	18	41	56	−15	36
19	Blackburn Rovers	38	7	14	17	38	52	−14	35
20	Nottingham Forest	38	7	9	22	35	69	−34	30

SEASON STATS

League Position: 2nd

Managers: Arsene Wenger

Top Goalscorer: Nicolas Anelka (17)

Most Assists: Dennis Bergkamp (13)

Most Appearances: Marc Overmars (37)

Biggest Win: MID 1–6 ARS (A)

Heaviest Defeat: AVL 3–2 ARS (A)

1999–2000

1	Manchester United (C)	38	28	7	3	97	45	52	91
2	Arsenal	38	22	7	9	73	43	30	73
3	Leeds United	38	21	6	11	58	43	15	69
4	Liverpool	38	19	10	9	51	30	21	67
5	Chelsea	38	18	11	9	53	34	19	65
6	Aston Villa	38	15	13	10	46	35	11	58
7	Sunderland	38	16	10	12	57	56	1	58
8	Leicester City	38	16	7	15	55	55	0	55
9	West Ham United	38	15	10	13	52	53	–1	55
10	Tottenham Hotspur	38	15	8	15	57	49	8	53

11	Newcastle United	38	14	10	14	63	54	9	52
12	Middlesbrough	38	14	10	14	46	52	−6	52
13	Everton	38	12	14	12	59	49	10	50
14	Coventry City	38	12	8	18	47	54	−7	44
15	Southampton	38	12	8	18	45	62	−17	44
16	Derby County	38	9	11	18	44	57	−13	38
17	Bradford City	38	9	9	20	38	68	−30	36
18	Wimbledon (R)	38	7	12	19	46	74	−28	33
19	Sheffield Wednesday (R)	38	8	7	23	38	70	−32	31
20	Watford (R)	38	6	6	26	35	77	−42	24

SEASON STATS

League Position: 2nd

Managers: Arsene Wenger

Top Goalscorer: Thierry Henry (17)

Most Assists: Dennis Bergkamp (9)

Most Appearances: Thierry Henry (31)
Kanu (31)
Sylvinho (31)
Marc Overmars (31)

Biggest Win: ARS 5–1 MID (H)

Heaviest Defeat: NEW 4–2 ARS (A)

2000–01

1	Manchester United (C)	38	24	8	6	79	31	48	80
2	Arsenal	38	20	10	8	63	38	25	70
3	Liverpool	38	20	9	9	71	39	32	69
4	Leeds United	38	20	8	10	64	43	21	68
5	Ipswich Town	38	20	6	12	57	42	15	66
6	Chelsea	38	17	10	11	68	45	23	61
7	Sunderland	38	15	12	11	46	41	5	57
8	Aston Villa	38	13	15	10	46	43	3	54
9	Charlton Athletic	38	14	10	14	50	57	−7	52
10	Southampton	38	14	10	14	40	48	−8	52
11	Newcastle United	38	14	9	15	44	50	−6	51
12	Tottenham Hotspur	38	13	10	15	47	54	−7	49
13	Leicester City	38	14	6	18	39	51	−12	48
14	Middlesbrough	38	9	15	14	44	44	0	42
15	West Ham United	38	10	12	16	45	50	−5	42
16	Everton	38	11	9	18	45	59	−14	42
17	Derby County	38	10	12	1§6	37	59	−22	42
18	Manchester City (R)	38	8	10	20	41	65	−24	34
19	Coventy City (R)	38	8	10	29	36	63	−27	34
20	Bradford City (R)	38	5	11	22	30	70	−40	26

SEASON STATS

League Position: 2nd

Managers: Arsene Wenger

Top Goalscorer: Thierry Henry (17)

Most Assists: Thierry Henry (9)

Most Appearances: Thierry Henry (35)

Biggest Win: ARS 6–1 LEI (H)

Heaviest Defeat: MUN 6–1 ARS (A)

2001–02

1	Arsenal (C)	38	26	9	3	79	36	32	87
2	Liverpool	38	24	8	6	67	30	37	80
3	Manchester United	38	24	5	9	87	45	42	77
4	Newcastle United	38	21	8	9	74	52	22	71
5	Leeds United	38	18	12	8	53	37	16	66
6	Chelsea	38	17	13	8	66	38	28	64
7	West Ham United	38	15	8	15	48	57	–9	53
8	Aston Villa	38	12	14	12	46	47	–1	50
9	Tottenham Hotspur	38	14	8	16	49	53	–4	50
10	Blackburn Rovers	38	12	10	16	55	51	4	46

11	Southampton	38	12	9	17	46	54	−8	45
12	Middlesbrough	38	12	9	17	35	47	−12	44
13	Fulham	38	10	14	14	36	44	−8	44
14	Charlton Athletic	38	10	14	14	38	49	−11	44
15	Everton	38	11	10	17	45	57	−12	43
16	Bolton Wanderers	38	9	13	16	44	62	−18	40
17	Sunderland	38	10	10	18	29	51	−22	40
18	Ipswich Town (R)	38	9	9	20	41	64	−23	36
19	Derby County (R)	38	8	6	24	33	63	−30	30
20	Leicester City (R)	38	5	13	20	30	64	−34	28

SEASON STATS

League Position: 1st

Managers: Arsene Wenger

Top Goalscorer: Thierry Henry (24)

Most Assists: Robert Pires (15)

Most Appearances: Patrick Vieira (36)

Biggest Win: MID 0–4 ARS (A)

Heaviest Defeat: ARS 2–4 CHA (H)

2002–03

1	Manchester United (C)	38	25	8	5	74	34	40	83
2	Arsenal	38	23	9	6	85	42	43	78
3	Newcastle United	38	21	6	11	63	48	15	69
4	Chelsea	38	199	10	9	68	38	30	67
5	Liverpool	38	18	10	10	61	41	20	64
6	Blackburn Rovers	38	16	12	10	52	43	9	60
7	Everton	38	17	8	13	48	49	−1	59
8	Southampton	38	13	13	12	43	46	−3	52
9	Manchester City	38	15	6	17	47	54	−7	51
10	Tottenham Hotspur	38	14	8	16	51	62	−11	50
11	Middlesbrough	38	13	10	15	48	44	4	49
12	Charlton Athletic	38	14	7	17	45	56	−11	49
13	Birmingham City	38	13	9	16	41	49	−8	48
14	Fulham	38	13	9	16	41	50	−9	48
15	Leeds United	38	14	5	19	58	57	1	47
16	Aston Villa	38	12	9	17	42	47	−5	45
17	Bolton Wanderers	38	10	14	14	41	51	−10	44
18	West Ham United (R)	38	10	12	16	42	59	−17	42
19	West Bromwich Albion (R)	38	6	8	24	29	65	−36	26
20	Sunderland (R)	38	4	7	27	21	65	−44	19

SEASON STATS

League Position: 2nd

Managers: Arsene Wenger

Top Goalscorer: Thierry Henry (24)

Most Assists: Thierry Henry (20)

Most Appearances: Thierry Henry (37)

Biggest Win: ARS 6–1 SOU (H)

Heaviest Defeat: 2–0 v. BLA(A) & MNU (A)

2003–04

1	Arsenal (C)	38	26	12	0	73	26	47	90
2	Chelsea	38	24	7	7	67	30	37	79
3	Manchester United	38	23	6	9	64	35	29	75
4	Liverpool	38	16	12	10	55	37	18	60
5	Newcastle United	38	13	17	8	52	40	12	56
6	Aston Villa	38	15	11	12	48	44	4	56
7	Charlton Athletic	38	14	11	13	51	51	0	53
8	Bolton Wanderers	38	14	11	13	48	56	–8	53
9	Fulham	38	14	10	14	52	46	6	52
10	Birmingham City	38	12	14	12	43	48	–5	50

11	Middlesbrough	38	13	9	16	44	52	−8	48
12	Southampton	38	12	11	15	44	45	−1	44
13	Portsmouth	38	12	9	17	47	54	−7	45
14	Tottenham Hotspur	38	13	6	19	47	57	−10	45
15	Blackburn Rovers	38	12	8	18	51	59	−8	44
16	Manchester City	38	9	14	15	55	54	1	41
17	Everton	38	9	12	17	45	57	−12	39
18	Leicester City (R)	38	6	15	17	48	65	−17	33
19	Leeds United (R)	38	8	9	21	40	79	−39	33
20	Wolverhampton Wanderers (R)	38	7	12	19	38	77	−39	33

SEASON STATS

League Position: 1st

Managers: Arsene Wenger

Top Goalscorer: Thierry Henry (30)

Most Assists: Robert Pires (8)

Most Appearances: Jens Lehmann (38)

Biggest Win: ARS 5–0 LEE (H)

Heaviest Defeat: Not Applicable

2004–05

1	Chelsea (C)	38	29	8	1	72	15	57	95
2	Arsenal	38	25	8	5	87	36	51	83
3	Manchester United	38	22	11	5	58	26	32	77
4	Everton	38	18	7	13	45	46	−1	61
5	Liverpool	38	17	7	14	52	41	11	58
6	Bolton Wanderers	38	16	10	12	49	44	5	58
7	Middlesbrough	38	14	13	11	53	46	7	55
8	Manchester City	38	13	13	12	47	39	8	52
9	Tottenham Hotspur	38	14	10	14	47	41	6	52
10	Aston Villa	38	12	11	15	45	52	−7	47
11	Charlton Athletic	38	12	10	16	42	58	−16	46
12	Birmingham City	38	11	12	15	40	46	−6	45
13	Fulham	38	12	8	18	51	60	−8	44
14	Newcastle United	38	10	14	14	47	57	−10	44
15	Blackburn Rovers	38	9	15	14	32	43	−11	42
16	Portsmouth	38	10	9	19	43	59	−16	39
17	West Bromwich Albion	38	6	16	16	36	61	−25	34
18	Crystal Palace (R)	38	7	12	19	41	62	−21	33
19	Norwich City (R)	38	7	12	19	42	77	−35	33
20	Southampton (R)	38	6	14	18	45	66	−21	32

SEASON STATS

League Position: 2nd

Managers: Arsene Wenger

Top Goalscorer: Thierry Henry (25)

Most Assists: Thierry Henry (14)

Most Appearances: Ashley Cole (35)
Kolo Toure (35)

Biggest Win: ARS 7–0 EVE (H)

Heaviest Defeat: ARS 2–4 MUN (H)

2005–06

1	Chelsea (C)	38	29	4	5	72	22	50	91
2	Manchester United	38	25	8	5	72	34	38	83
3	Liverpool	38	25	7	6	57	25	32	82
4	Arsenal	38	20	7	11	68	31	37	67
5	Tottenham Hotspur	38	18	11	9	53	38	15	65
6	Blackburn Rovers	38	19	6	13	51	41	9	62
7	Newcastle United	38	17	7	14	47	42	5	58
8	Bolton Wanderers	38	15	11	12	49	41	8	56
9	West Ham United	38	16	7	15	51	55	–3	55
10	Wigan Athletic	38	15	6	17	45	52	–7	51

11	Everton	38	14	8	16	34	49	−15	50
12	Fulham	38	14	6	18	48	58	−10	48
13	Charlton Athletic	38	13	8	17	41	55	-14	47
14	Middlesbrough	38	12	9	17	48	58	−10	45
15	Manchester City	38	13	4	21	43	48	−5	43
16	Aston Villa	38	10	12	16	42	55	−13	42
17	Portsmouth	38	10	8	20	37	62	−25	38
18	Birmingham City (R)	38	8	10	20	28	50	−22	34
19	West Bromwich Albion (R)	38	7	9	22	31	58	−27	30
20	Sunderland (R)	38	3	6	29	26	69	−43	15

SEASON STATS

League Position: 4th

Managers: Arsene Wenger

Top Goalscorer: Thierry Henry (27)

Most Assists: Jose Antonio Reyes (10)

Most Appearances: Jens Lehmann (38)

Biggest Win: ARS 7–0 MID (H)

Heaviest Defeat: 2–0 v. BOL (A) & MNU (A)

2006–07

1	Manchester United (C)	38	28	5	5	83	27	56	89
2	Chelsea	38	24	11	3	64	24	40	83
3	Liverpool	38	20	8	10	57	27	30	68
4	Arsenal	38	19	11	8	63	35	28	68
5	Tottenham Hotspur	38	17	9	12	57	54	3	60
6	Everton	38	15	13	10	52	36	16	58
7	Bolton Wanderers	38	16	8	14	47	52	−5	56
8	Reading	38	16	7	15	52	47	5	55
9	Portsmouth	38	14	12	12	45	42	3	54
10	Blackburn Rovers	38	15	7	16	52	54	−2	52
11	Aston Villa	38	11	17	10	43	41	2	50
12	Middlesbrough	38	12	10	16	44	19	−5	46
13	Newcastle United	38	11	10	17	38	47	−9	43
14	Manchester City	38	11	9	18	29	44	−15	42
15	West Ham United	38	12	5	21	35	59	−24	41
16	Fulham	38	8	15	15	38	60	−22	39
17	Wigan Athletic	38	10	8	20	37	59	−22	38
18	Sheffield United (R)	38	10	8	20	32	55	−23	38
19	Charlton Athletic (R)	38	8	10	20	34	60	−26	34
20	Watford (R)	38	5	13	20	29	59	−30	28

SEASON STATS

League Position: 4th

Managers: Arsene Wenger

Top Goalscorer: Robin van Persie (11)

Most Assists: Cesc Fabregas (11)

Most Appearances: Cesc Fabregas (38)

Biggest Win: ARS 6–2 BLB (H)

Heaviest Defeat: LIV 4–1 ARS (A)

2007–08

1	Manchester United (C)	38	27	6	5	80	22	58	87
2	Chelsea	38	25	10	3	65	26	39	85
3	Arsenal	38	24	11	3	74	31	43	83
4	Liverpool	38	21	13	4	67	28	39	76
5	Everton	38	19	8	11	55	33	22	65
6	Aston Villa	38	16	12	10	71	51	20	60
7	Blackburn Rovers	38	15	13	10	50	48	2	58
8	Portsmouth	38	16	9	13	48	40	8	57
9	Manchester City	38	15	10	13	45	53	–8	55
10	West Ham United	38	13	10	15	42	50	–8	49

11	Tottenham Hotspur	38	11	13	14	66	61	5	46
12	Newcastle United	38	11	10	17	45	65	−20	43
13	Middlesbrough	38	10	12	16	43	53	−10	42
14	Wigan Athletic	38	10	10	18	34	51	−17	40
15	Sunderland	38	11	6	21	36	59	−23	39
16	Bolton Wanderers	38	9	10	19	36	54	−18	37
17	Fulham	38	8	12	18	38	60	−22	36
18	Reading (R)	38	10	6	22	41	66	−25	36
19	Birmingham City (R)	38	8	11	19	46	62	−16	35
20	Derby County (R)	38	1	8	29	20	89	−69	11

SEASON STATS

League Position: 3rd

Managers: Arsene Wenger

Top Goalscorer: Emmanuel Adebayor (24)

Most Assists: Cesc Fabregas (17)

Most Appearances: Gael Clichy (38)

Biggest Win: ARS 5–0 DER (H)

Heaviest Defeat: 2–1 v. CHE(A), MNU(A)& MID(A)

2008–09

1	Manchester United (C)	38	28	6	4	68	24	44	90
2	Liverpool	38	25	11	2	77	27	50	86
3	Chelsea	38	25	8	5	68	24	44	83
4	Arsenal	38	20	12	6	68	37	31	72
5	Everton	38	17	12	9	55	37	18	63
6	Aston Villa	38	17	11	10	54	48	6	62
7	Fulham	38	14	11	13	39	34	5	53
8	Tottenham Hotspur	38	14	9	15	45	45	0	51
9	West Ham United	38	14	9	15	42	45	–3	51
10	Manchester City	38	15	5	18	58	50	8	50
11	Wigan Athletic	38	12	9	17	34	45	–11	45
12	Stoke City	38	12	9	17	38	55	–17	45
13	Bolton Wanderers	38	11	8	19	41	53	–12	41
14	Portsmouth	38	10	11	17	38	57	–19	41
15	Blackburn Rovers	38	10	11	17	40	60	–20	41
16	Sunderland	38	9	9	20	34	54	–20	36
17	Hull City	38	8	11	19	39	64	–25	35
18	Newcastle United (R)	38	7	13	18	40	59	–10	34
19	Middlesbrough (R)	38	7	11	20	28	57	–29	32
20	West Bromwich Albion (R)	38	8	8	22	36	67	–31	32

SEASON STATS

League Position: 4th

Managers: Arsene Wenger

Top Goalscorer: Robin van Persie (11)

Most Assists: Robin van Persie (10)

Most Appearances: Denilson (37)

Biggest Win: BLB 0–4 ARS (A)

Heaviest Defeat: ARS 1–4 CHE (H)

2009–10

1	Chelsea (C)	38	27	5	6	103	32	71	86
2	Manchester United	38	27	4	7	86	28	58	85
3	Arsenal	38	23	6	9	83	41	42	75
4	Tottenham Hotspur	38	21	7	10	67	41	26	70
5	Manchester City	38	18	13	7	73	45	28	67
6	Aston Villa	38	17	13	8	52	39	13	64
7	Liverpool	38	18	9	11	61	35	26	63
8	Everton	38	16	13	9	60	49	11	61
9	Birmingham City	38	13	11	14	38	47	–9	50
10	Blackburn Rovers	38	13	11	14	41	55	–14	50

11	Stoke City	38	11	14	13	34	48	−14	47
12	Fulham	38	12	10	16	39	46	−7	46
13	Sunderland	38	11	11	16	48	56	−8	44
14	Bolton Wanderers	38	10	9	19	42	67	−25	39
15	Wolverhampton Wanderers	38	9	11	18	32	56	−24	38
16	Wigan Athletic	38	9	9	20	37	79	−42	36
17	West Ham United	38	8	11	19	47	66	−19	35
18	Burnley (R)	38	8	6	24	42	82	−40	30
19	Hull City (R)	38	6	12	20	34	75	−41	30
20	Portsmouth (R)	38	7	7	24	34	66	−32	19

SEASON STATS

League Position: 3rd

Managers: Arsene Wenger

Top Goalscorer: Cesc Fabregas (15)

Most Assists: Cesc Fabregas (13)

Most Appearances: Bacary Sagna (35)

Biggest Win: EVE 1–6 ARS (A)

Heaviest Defeat: ARS 0–3 CHE (H)

2010–11

1	Manchester United (C)	38	23	11	4	78	37	41	80
2	Chelsea	38	21	8	9	69	33	36	71
3	Manchester City	38	21	8	9	60	33	27	71
4	Arsenal	38	19	11	8	72	43	29	68
5	Tottenham Hotspur	38	16	14	8	55	46	9	62
6	Liverpool	38	17	7	14	59	44	15	58
7	Everton	38	13	15	10	51	45	6	54
8	Fulham	38	11	16	11	49	43	6	49
9	Aston Villa	38	12	12	14	48	59	−11	48
10	Sunderland	38	12	11	15	45	56	−11	47
11	West Bromwich Albion	38	12	11	15	56	71	−15	47
12	Newcastle United	38	11	13	14	56	57	−1	46
13	Stoke City	38	13	7	18	46	48	−2	46
14	Bolton Wanderers	38	12	10	16	52	56	−4	46
15	Blackburn Rovers	38	11	10	17	46	59	−13	43
16	Wigan Athletic	38	9	15	14	40	61	−21	42
17	Wolverhampton Wanderers	38	11	7	20	46	66	−20	40
18	Birmingham City (R)	38	8	15	15	37	58	−21	39
19	Blackpool (R)	38	10	9	19	55	78	−23	39
20	West Ham United (R)	38	7	12	19	43	79	−27	33

SEASON STATS

League Position: 4th

Managers: Arsene Wenger

Top Goalscorer: Robin van Persie (18)

Most Assists: Andrey Arshavin (11)

Most Appearances: Andrey Arshavin (37)

Biggest Win: ARS 6–0 BLP (H)

Heaviest Defeat: STK 3–1 ARS (A)

2011–12

1	Manchester City (C)	38	28	5	5	93	29	64	89
2	Manchester United	38	28	5	5	89	33	56	89
3	Arsenal	38	21	7	10	74	49	25	70
4	Tottenham Hotspur	38	20	9	9	66	41	25	69
5	Newcastle United	38	19	8	11	56	51	5	65
6	Chelsea	38	18	10	10	65	46	19	64
7	Everton	38	15	11	12	50	40	10	56
8	Liverpool	38	14	10	14	47	40	7	52
9	Fulham	38	14	10	14	48	51	–3	52
10	West Bromwich Albion	38	13	8	17	45	52	–7	47

11	Swansea City	38	12	11	15	44	51	−7	47
12	Norwich City	38	12	11	15	52	66	−14	47
13	Sunderland	38	11	12	15	45	46	−1	45
14	Stoke City	38	11	12	15	36	53	−17	45
15	Wigan Athletic	38	11	10	17	42	62	−20	43
16	Aston Villa	38	7	17	14	37	53	−16	38
17	Queens Park Rangers	38	10	7	21	43	66	−23	37
18	Bolton Wanderers (R)	38	10	6	22	46	77	−31	36
19	Blackburn Rovers (R)	38	8	7	23	48	78	−30	31
20	Wolverhampton Wanderers (R)	38	5	10	23	40	82	−42	25

SEASON STATS

League Position: 3rd

Managers: Arsene Wenger

Top Goalscorer: Robin van Persie (30)

Most Assists: Alexandre Song (11)

Most Appearances: Wojciech Szczesny (38)
Robin van Persie (38)

Biggest Win: ARS 7–1 BLB (H)

Heaviest Defeat: MUN 8–2 ARS (A)

Career Record

2012–13

1	Manchester United (C)	38	28	5	5	86	43	43	89
2	Manchester City	38	23	9	6	66	34	32	78
3	Chelsea	38	22	9	7	75	39	36	75
4	Arsenal	38	21	110	7	72	37	35	73
5	Tottenham Hotspur	38	21	9	8	66	46	20	72
6	Everton	38	16	15	7	55	40	15	63
7	Liverpool	38	16	13	9	71	43	28	61
8	West Bromwich Albion	38	14	7	17	53	57	–4	49
9	Swansea City	38	11	13	14	47	51	–4	46
10	West Ham United	38	12	10	16	45	53	–8	46
11	Norwich City	38	10	14	14	41	58	–17	44
12	Fulham	38	11	10	17	50	60	–10	43
13	Stoke City	38	9	15	14	34	45	–11	42
14	Southampton	38	9	14	15	49	60	–11	41
15	Aston Villa	38	10	11	17	47	69	–22	41
16	Newcastle United	38	11	8	19	45	68	–23	41
17	Sunderland	38	9	12	17	41	54	–13	39
18	Wigan Athletic (R)	38	9	9	20	47	73	–26	36
19	Reading (R)	38	6	10	22	43	73	–30	28
20	QPR (R)	38	4	13	21	30	60	–35	25

SEASON STATS

League Position: 4th

Managers: Arsene Wenger

Top Goalscorer: Theo Walcott (14)

Most Assists: Santi Cazorla (11)

Most Appearances: Santi Cazorla (38)

Biggest Win: ARS 6–1 SOU (H)

Heaviest Defeat: 0–2 v. MCN (H) & SWA (H)

2013–14

1	Manchester City (C)	38	27	5	6	102	37	65	86
2	Liverpool	38	26	6	6	101	50	51	84
3	Chelsea	38	25	7	6	71	27	44	82
4	Arsenal	38	24	7	7	68	41	27	79
5	Everton	38	21	99	8	61	39	22	72
6	Tottenham Hotspur	38	21	6	11	55	51	4	69
7	Manchester United	38	19	7	12	64	43	21	64
8	Southampton	38	15	11	12	54	46	8	56
9	Stoke City	38	13	11	14	45	52	−7	50
10	Newcastle United	38	15	4	19	43	59	−16	49

11	Crystal Palace	38	13	6	19	33	48	−15	45
12	Swansea City	38	11	9	18	54	54	0	42
13	West Ham United	38	11	7	20	40	51	−11	40
14	Sunderland	38	10	8	20	41	60	−19	38
15	Aston Villa	38	10	8	20	39	61	−22	38
16	Hull City	38	10	7	21	38	53	−15	37
17	West Bromwich Albion	38	8	12	18	43	59	−16	36
18	Norwich City (R)	38	8	9	21	28	62	−34	33
19	Fulham(R)	38	9	5	24	40	85	−45	32
20	Cardiff (R)	38	7	9	22	32	74	−42	30

SEASON STATS

League Position: 4th

Managers: Arsene Wenger

Top Goalscorer: Olivier Giroud (16)

Most Assists: Mesut Ozil (9)

Most Appearances: Wojciech Szczesny (37)

Biggest Win: ARS 4–1 NOR (H)

Heaviest Defeat: CHE 6–0 ARS (A)

2014–15

1	Chelsea (C)	38	26	9	3	73	32	41	87
2	Manchester City	38	24	7	7	83	38	45	79
3	Arsenal	38	22	9	7	71	36	35	75
4	Manchester United	38	20	10	8	62	37	25	70
5	Tottenham Hotspur	38	19	7	12	58	53	5	64
6	Liverpool	38	18	8	12	52	48	4	62
7	Southampton	38	18	6	14	54	33	21	60
8	Swansea City	38	16	8	14	46	49	–3	56
9	Stoke City	38	15	9	14	48	45	3	54
10	Crystal Palace	38	13	9	16	47	51	–4	48
11	Everton	38	12	11	15	48	50	–2	47
12	West Ham United	38	12	11	15	44	47	–3	47
13	West Bromwich Albion	38	11	11	16	38	51	–13	44
14	Leicester City	38	11	8	19	46	55	–9	41
15	Newcastle United	38	10	9	19	40	63	–23	39
16	Sunderland	38	7	17	14	31	53	–22	38
17	Aston Villa	38	10	8	20	31	57	–26	38
18	Hull City (R)	38	8	11	19	33	51	–18	35
19	Burnley (R)	38	7	12	19	28	53	–25	33
20	Queens Park Rangers (R)	38	8	6	24	42	73	–31	30

Career Record

SEASON STATS

League Position: 3rd

Managers: Arsene Wenger

Top Goalscorer: Alexis Sanchez (16)

Most Assists: Santi Cazorla (11)

Most Appearances: Santi Cazorla (37)

Biggest Win: ARS 5–0 AVL (H)

Heaviest Defeat: 0–2 v. CHE (A) & SOT (A)

2015–16

1	Leicester City (C)	38	23	12	3	68	36	32	81
2	Arsenal	38	20	11	7	65	36	29	71
3	Tottenham Hotspur	38	19	13	6	69	35	34	70
4	Manchester City	38	19	9	10	71	41	30	66
5	Manchester United	38	19	9	10	49	35	14	66
6	Southampton	38	18	9	11	59	41	18	63
7	West Ham United	38	16	14	8	65	51	14	62
8	Liverpool	38	16	12	10	63	50	13	60
9	Stoke City	38	14	9	15	41	55	–14	51
10	Chelsea	38	12	14	12	59	53	6	50

11	Everton	38	11	14	13	59	55	4	47
12	Swansea City	38	12	11	15	42	52	−10	47
13	Watford	38	12	9	17	40	50	−10	45
14	West Bromwich Albion	38	10	13	15	34	48	−14	43
15	Crystal Palace	38	11	9	18	39	51	−12	42
16	Bournemouth	38	11	9	18	45	67	−22	42
17	Sunderland	38	9	12	17	48	62	−14	39
18	Newcastle United (R)	38	9	10	19	44	65	−21	37
19	Norwich City(R)	38	9	7	22	39	67	−28	34
20	Aston Villa (R)	38	3	8	27	27	76	−49	17

SEASON STATS

League Position: 2nd

Managers: Arsene Wenger

Top Goalscorer: Olivier Giroud (16)

Most Assists: Mesut Ozil (19)

Most Appearances: Olivier Giroud (38)

Biggest Win: ARS 4–0 WAT (H) & AST (H)

Heaviest Defeat: SOU 4–0 ARS (A)

2016–17

1	Chelsea (C)	38	30	3	5	85	33	52	93
2	Tottenham Hotspur	38	26	8	4	86	26	60	86
3	Manchester City	38	23	9	6	80	39	41	78
4	Liverpool	38	22	10	6	78	42	36	76
5	Arsenal	38	23	6	9	77	44	33	75
6	Manchester United	38	18	15	5	54	29	25	69
7	Everton	38	17	10	11	62	44	18	61
8	Southampton	38	12	10	16	41	48	–7	46
9	Bournemouth	38	12	10	16	55	67	–12	46
10	West Bromwich Albion	38	12	9	17	43	51	–8	45
11	West Ham United	38	12	9	17	47	64	–17	45
12	Leicester City	38	12	8	18	48	63	–15	44
13	Stoke City	38	11	11	16	41	56	–15	44
14	Crystal Palace	38	12	5	21	50	63	–13	41
15	Swansea City	38	12	5	21	45	70	–25	41
16	Burnley	38	11	7	20	39	55	–16	40
17	Watford	38	11	7	20	40	68	–28	40
18	Hull City (R)	38	9	7	22	37	80	–43	34
19	Middlesborough (R)	38	5	13	20	27	53	–26	28
20	Sunderland (R)	38	6	6	26	29	69	–40	24

SEASON STATS

League Position: 5th

Managers: Arsene Wenger

Top Goalscorer: Alexis Sanchez (24)

Most Assists: Alexis Sanchez (10)

Most Appearances: Alexis Sanchez (38)

Biggest Win: WHU 1–5 ARS (A)

Heaviest Defeat: CRY 3–0 ARS (A)

2017–18

1	Manchester City (C)	38	32	4	2	106	27	79	100
2	Manchester United	38	25	6	7	68	28	40	81
3	Tottenham Hotspur	38	23	8	7	74	36	38	77
4	Liverpool	38	21	12	5	84	38	46	75
5	Chelsea	38	21	7	10	62	38	24	70
6	Arsenal	38	19	6	13	74	51	23	63
7	Burnley	38	14	12	12	36	39	–3	54
8	Everton	38	13	10	15	44	58	–14	49
9	Leicester City	38	12	11	15	56	60	–4	47
10	Newcastle United	38	12	8	18	39	47	–8	44

11	Crystal Palace	38	11	11	16	45	55	−10	44
12	Bournemouth	38	11	11	16	45	61	−16	44
13	West Ham United	38	10	12	16	48	68	−20	42
14	Watford	38	11	8	19	44	64	−20	41
15	Brighton & Hove Albion	38	9	13	16	34	54	−20	40
16	Huddersfield Town	38	9	10	19	28	58	−30	37
17	Southampton	38	7	15	16	37	56	−19	36
18	Swansea City (R)	38	8	9	21	28	56	−28	33
19	Stoke City(R)	38	7	12	19	35	68	−33	33
20	West Bromwich Albion (R)	38	6	13	19	31	56	−25	31

SEASON STATS

League Position: 6th

Managers: Arsene Wenger

Top Goalscorer: Alexandre Lacazette (14)

Most Assists: Mesut Ozil (8)

Most Appearances: Granit Xhaka (38)

Biggest Win: ARS 5–0 HUD (H) & AST (H)

Heaviest Defeat: LIV 4–0 ARS (A)

Source for all tables: premierleague.com/tables

BY THE NUMBERS

Games on penalties are counted as wins or losses. UEFA Champions League games include qualifiers.

MATCHES MANAGED – 1235

Premier League:
828 games, 476 wins, 199 draws, 153 loses.

UEFA Champions League:
191 games, 96 wins, 42 draws, 53 losses

FA Cup:
109 games, 78 wins, 16 draws, 15 losses

League Cup:
73 games, 45 wins, 4 draws, 24 losses

UEFA Cup/Europa League:
25 games, 14 wins, 5 draws, 6 losses

FA Community Shield:
9 games, 7 wins, 2 losses

FINAL LEAGUE POSITION AT ARSENAL

First: 3, **Second**: 6, **Third**: 5, **Fourth**: 6, **Fifth**: 1

ARSENE WENGER AT HIGHBURY
& THE EMIRATES STADIUM

Stadium	Matches Played	Wins	Draws	Losses	Goals For	Goals Against	Win %	GF/ game	GA/ game
Highbury	265	186	53	26	574	218	70.2%	2.17	0.82
Emirates	333	226	65	42	709	264	67.9%	2.13	0.79

Arsene Wenger has won a Premier League game on his birthday three times (2005, 2006, 2017); more often than any other manager.

Arsenal have played 124 opponents and failed to beat only five of them: Fiorentina, PAOK Salonika, Paris Saint-Germain, Port Vale and Rotherham United.

1–0 was Wenger's third most common scoreline in Arsenal games in all competitions (124), after 1–1 and 2–1 (127 each).

In 1997–98, Arsene Wenger became the first non-British manager to win the English top flight since the inauguration of the second tier in 1892–93.

Arsene Wenger oversaw 10 wins in 10 games against Reading in all competitions; his best 100% record against a single club as Arsenal manager.

MOST GOALS FOR ARSENAL UNDER ARSENE WENGER

Thierry Henry, 228

Robin van Persie, 132

Theo Walcott, 108

Olivier Giroud, 105

Dennis Bergkamp, 102

Robert Pires, 84

Alexis Sanchez, 80

Freddie Ljungberg, 72

Emmanuel Adebayor, 62

Aaron Ramsey, 58

LANDMARK GOALS

1. Ian Wright v. Blackburn Rovers 12 October 1996, 1st goal scored while Wenger managed Arsenal
2. Tony Adams v. Leicester City 12 April 1994, 50th goal
3. Marc Overmars v. Leeds United 10 January 1998, 100th goal
4. Thierry Henry v. Watford 5 January 2002, 500th goal
5. Jose Antonio Reyes v. Manchester City 4 May 2006, 1000th goal
6. Olivier Giroud v. Swansea City 31 October 2015, 2000th goal

MOST PREMIER LEAGUE MATCHES AS MANAGER

Manager	Matches Played	Wins	Draws	Losses	Goals for	Goals against
Arsène Wenger	828	476	199	153	1561	807
Alex Ferguson	810	528	168	114	1627	703
Harry Redknapp	641	236	167	238	818	846
David Moyes	545	209	149	187	718	687
Sam Allardyce	512	174	138	200	606	698
Mark Hughes	466	158	127	181	572	643
Steve Bruce	430	121	120	189	440	573
Martin O'Neill	359	130	115	114	474	447
Rafael Benitez	340	168	82	90	519	316
Alan Curbishley	328	108	85	135	381	472

THE INVINCIBLES: ARSENAL'S 49-GAME UNBEATEN RECORD

Arsenal went a record 49 consecutive top-flight league games unbeaten from May 2003 to October 2004, breaking Nottingham Forest's previous record of 42 set between November 1977 and November 1978.

In completing this remarkable run, Arsenal also recorded an unbeaten top-flight league season, only equalled by Preston North End who went the season unbeaten in 1888–89.

Career Record

	Played	Wins	Draws	Losses	Goals For	Goals Against	Goal Difference	Points
Home	25	20	5	0	63	21	42	65
Away	24	16	8	0	49	14	35	56
Overall	49	36	13	0	112	35	77	121

FORM GUIDE

W-W-W-W-W-W-D-D-W-W
W-D-W-W-W-D-D-W-D-W
W-D-W-W-W-W-W-W-W-W
W-D-W-D-W-D-D-D-W-W
W-W-W-W-W-D-W-W-W-L

SEASON 2002–03

1. 7 May 2003: Arsenal 6–1 Southampton
2. 11 May 2003: Sunderland 0–4 Arsenal

SEASON 2003–04

3. 16 August 2003: Arsenal 2–1 Everton
4. 24 August 2003: Middlesbrough 0–4 Arsenal

5. 27 August 2003: Arsenal 2–0 Aston Villa

6. 31 August 2003: Manchester City 1–2 Arsenal

7. 13 September 2003: Arsenal 1–1 Portsmouth

8. 21 September 2003: Manchester United 0–0 Arsenal

9. 26 September 2003: Arsenal 3–2 Newcastle United

10. 4 October 2003: Liverpool 1–2 Arsenal

11. 18 October 2003: Arsenal 2–1 Chelsea

12. 26 October 2003: Charlton Athletic 1–1 Arsenal

13. 1 November 2003: Leeds United 1–4 Arsenal

14. 8 November 2003: Arsenal 2–1 Tottenham Hotspur

15. 22 November 2003: Birmingham City 0–3 Arsenal

16. 30 November 2003: Arsenal 0–0 Fulham

17. 6 December 2003: Leicester City 1–1 Arsenal

18. 14 December 2003: Arsenal 1–0 Blackburn Rovers

19. 20 December 2003: Bolton Wanderers 1–1 Arsenal

20. 26 December 2003: Arsenal 3–0 Wolverhampton
    Wanderers

21. 29 December 2003: Southampton 0–1 Arsenal

22. 7 January 2004: Everton 1–1 Arsenal

23. 10 January 2004: Arsenal 4–1 Middlesbrough

24. 18 January 2004: Aston Villa 0–2 Arsenal

25. 1 February 2004: Arsenal 2–1 Manchester City

26. 7 February 2004: Wolverhampton Wanderers 1–3
    Arsenal

27. 10 February 2004: Arsenal 2–0 Southampton

28. 21 February 2004: Chelsea 1–2 Arsenal

29. 28 February 2004: Arsenal 2–1 Charlton Athletic

30. 13 March 2004: Blackburn Rovers 0–2 Arsenal
31. 20 March 2004: Arsenal 2–1 Bolton Wanderers
32. 28 March 2004: Arsenal 1–1 Manchester United
33. 9 April 2004: Arsenal 4–2 Liverpool
34. 11 April 2004: Newcastle United 0–0 Arsenal
35. 16 April 2004: Arsenal 5–0 Leeds United
36. 25 April 2004: Tottenham Hotspur 2–2 Arsenal
37. 1 May 2004: Arsenal 0–0 Birmingham City
38. 4 May 2004: Portsmouth 1–1 Arsenal
39. 9 May 2004: Fulham 0–1 Arsenal
40. 15 May 2004: Arsenal 2–1 Leicester City

SEASON 2004–05

41. 15 August 2004: Everton 1–4 Arsenal
42. 22 August 2004: Arsenal 5–3 Middlesbrough
43. 25 August 2004: Arsenal 3–0 Blackburn Rovers
44. 28 August 2004: Norwich City 1–4 Arsenal
45. 11 September 2004: Fulham 0–3 Arsenal
46. 18 September 2004: Arsenal 2–2 Bolton Wanderers
47. 25 September 2004: Manchester City 0–1 Arsenal
48. 2 October 2004: Arsenal 4–0 Charlton Athletic
49. 16 October 2004: Arsenal 3–1 Aston Villa

Career Record

THE PLAYERS INVOLVED

Player	Starts	Substitute	Goals
Thierry Henry	48	–	39
Kolo Toure	47	1	1
Jens Lehmann	47	–	–
Robert Pires	40	5	23
Lauren	39	2	–
Sol Campbell	38	–	1
Gilberto	36	3	4
Freddie Ljungberg	35	4	10
Ashley Cole	35	–	1
Patrick Vieira	34	–	3
Dennis Bergkamp	29	10	7
Ray Parlour	18	9	–
Pascal Cygan	15	8	–
Edu	14	19	2
Jose Antonio Reyes	14	8	8
Gael Clichy	8	8	–
Sylvain Wiltord	8	4	3
Cesc Fabregas	6	2	1
Kanu	4	8	1
Martin Keown	3	7	–
Jeremie Aliadiere	3	7	-
Jermaine Pennant	2	5	3
Oleg Luzhny	2	–	–
Igor Stepanovs	2	–	–

Justin Hoyte	1	2	–
Giovanni van Bronckhorst	1	1	–
David Bentley	1	–	–
Ryan Garry	1	–	–
David Seaman	1	–	–
Stuart Taylor	1	–	–
Mathieu Flamini	–	5	–
Robin van Persie	–	3	–
Stathis Tavlaridis	–	1	–
Own goals	–	–	5

Club	Points average per season 1998-2018
Man U	80.0
Chelsea	76.0
Arsenal	75.7
Liverpool	67.3
Man City	60.9
Tottenham	58.7

BIG CLUBS

Arsene Wenger – Top Four Clubs Faced With Arsenal							
Opponent	Played	W	D	L	F	A	Win %
Chelsea	62	23	18	21	79	88	37.1%
Manchester United	60	18	15	27	69	85	30.0%
Liverpool	53	19	17	17	83	88	35.8%
Tottenham Hotspur	52	23	20	9	94	65	44.2%

(Source: Opta)

Manager	Played	W	D	L	F	A	Win %
Alex Ferguson	49	15	12	22	55	71	30.6%
Sam Allardyce	34	20	8	6	69	36	58.8%
David Moyes	34	22	8	4	69	28	64.7%
Harry Redknapp	33	16	13	4	67	34	48.5%
Mark Hughes	29	16	4	9	51	31	55.2%
Steve Bruce	27	19	6	2	52	13	70.4%
Rafael Benitez	24	10	6	8	40	35	41.7%
Martin O'Neill	21	10	9	2	31	16	47.6%
Tony Pulis	19	12	2	5	33	19	63.2%
Jose Mourinho	19	2	7	10	12	29	10.5%
Steve McClaren	18	15	0	3	46	11	83.3%
Alan Curbishley	17	12	2	3	33	12	70.6%
Claudio Ranieri	17	10	6	1	33	19	58.8%
Gerard Houllier	16	7	4	5	22	21	43.8%
Gordon Strachan	16	11	3	2	30	12	68.8%
Roberto Martinez	16	10	3	3	36	16	62.5%

Alan Pardew	16	9	5	2	33	16	56.3%
Graeme Souness	15	10	1	4	25	15	66.7%

(Source: Opta)

CHAMPIONSHIPS, TROPHIES, HONOURS, DISTINCTIONS

PLAYER
RC Strasbourg
Ligue 1: 1978–79

COACH
Monaco
Ligue 1: 1987–88
Coupe de France: 1990–91

Nagoya Grampus Eight
Emperor's Cup: 1995
Japanese Super Cup: 1996

Arsenal
Premier League: 1997–98, 2001–02, 2003–04
FA Cup: 1997–98, 2001–02, 2002–03, 2004–05, 2013–14, 2014–15, 2016–17
FA Charity/Community Shield: 1998, 1999, 2002, 2004, 2014, 2015, 2017

UEFA Champions League Runner-Up: 2005–06
UEFA Cup Runner-Up: 1999–2000

INDIVIDUAL HONOURS

J.League Manager of the Year: 1995
Onze d'Or Coach of The Year: 2000, 2002, 2003, 2004
Premier League Manager of the Season: 1997–98, 2001–02, 2003–04
LMA Manager of the Year: 2001–02, 2003–04
BBC Sports Personality of the Year Coach Award: 2002, 2004
London Football Awards: Outstanding Contribution to a London Club: 2015
World Manager of the Year: 1998
FWA Tribute Award: 2005
English Football Hall of Fame: 2006
France Football Manager of the Year: 2008
IFFHS World Coach of the Decade: 2001–10
Facebook FA Premier League Manager of the Year: 2014–15
Premier League Manager of the Month: March 1998, April 1998, October 2000, April 2002, September 2002, August 2003, February 2004, August 2004, September 2007, December 2007, February 2011, February 2012, September 2013, March 2015, October 2015

Career Record

France Football 32nd Greatest Manager of All Time: 2019
World Soccer 36th Greatest Manager of All Time: 2013
Laureus Lifetime Achievement Award: 2019

Source: 'Arsene Wenger', Wikipedia.

ARSENAL PLAYERS UNDER WENGER

Fifty-three nations have been represented in Arsene Wenger's first team. In the 110-year history of Arsenal prior to his arrival, only thirteen nations had been represented.

All 222 players to appear for Arsene Wenger, in order of first appearance.

Player	Starts and subs	Total
David Seaman	245	245
Martin Keown	250+14	264
Lee Dixon	207+18	225
Tony Adams	188	188
Steve Bould	81+12	93
Nigel Winterburn	155+11	166
Patrick Vieira	393+9	402
David Platt	41+27	68
Paul Merson	30	30
John Hartson	9+7	16
Ian Wright	56+3	59
Ray Parlour	270+48	318

Career Record

Dennis Bergkamp	298+78	376
Steve Morrow	2+11	13
Remi Garde	27+16	43
John Lukic	19	19
Andy Linighan	3+1	4
Paul Shaw	1+7	8
Gavin McGowan	1+1	2
Scott Marshall	8+5	13
Stephen Hughes	35+39	74
Matthew Rose	1	1
Lee Harper	1	1
Ian Selly	0+1	1
Nicolas Anelka	73+17	90
Gilles Grimandi	128+42	170
Emmanuel Petit	114+4	118
Marc Overmars	127+15	142
Luis Boa Morte	13+26	39
Christopher Wreh	18+28	46
Alex Manninger	63+1	64
Matthew Upson	39+17	56
Alberto Mendez	6+5	11
Paolo Vernazza	7+5	12
Jason Crowe	0+3	3
Jehad Muntasser	0+1	1
Isaiah Rankin	0+1	1
Nelson Vivas	29+40	69
Freddie Ljungberg	285+43	328
David Grondin	4	4

Omar Riza	0+1	1
Fabian Caballero	0+3	3
Michael Black	0+1	1
Kaba Diawara	3+12	15
Kanu	104+94	198
Silvinho	66+14	80
Oleg Luzhny	91+19	110
Thierry Henry	337+40	377
Davor Suker	15+24	39
Stefan Malz	6+8	14
Tommy Black	1+1	2
Rhys Weston	2+1	3
Jermaine Pennant	12+14	26
Ashley Cole	218+10	228
Graham Barrett	1+2	3
Brian McGovern	0+1	1
Julian Gray	0+1	1
Robert Pires	238+46	284
Lauren	227+14	241
Sylvain Wiltord	124+51	175
Igors Stepanovs	29+2	31
Stuart Taylor	26+4	30
Moritz Volz	1+1	2
Lee Cannoville	0+1	1
Tomas Danilevicius	0+3	3
Edu	76+51	127
Sol Campbell	208+3	211
Gio van Bronckhorst	39+25	64

Francis Jeffers	13+26	39
Junichi Inamoto	2+2	4
Richard Wright	22	22
Stathis Tavlaridis	7+1	8
John Halls	0+3	3
Rohan Ricketts	0+1	1
Carlin Itonga	0+1	1
Juan	2	2
Sebastian Svard	2+2	4
Jeremie Aliadiere	19+32	51
Gilberto	213+31	244
Kolo Toure	295+31	326
Pascal Cygan	80+18	98
Ryan Garry	1+1	2
Rami Shaaban	5	5
David Bentley	5+4	9
Justin Hoyte	50+18	68
Jens Lehmann	199+1	200
Graham Stack	5	5
Gael Clichy	230+34	264
Cesc Fabregas	266+37	303
Jerome Thomas	1+2	3
Ryan Smith	2+4	6
Quincy Owusu-Abeyie	8+15	23
John Spicer	0+1	1
Frankie Simek	1	1
Olafur-Ingi Skulason	0+1	1
Michal Papadopulos	0+1	1

Jose Antonio Reyes	89+21	110
Robin van Persie	211+67	278
Mathieu Flamini	174+72	246
Manuel Almunia	173+2	175
Sebastian Larsson	7+5	12
Arturo Lupoli	6+3	9
Philippe Senderos	105+12	117
Danny Karbassiyoon	1+2	3
Johan Djourou	123+21	144
Patrick Cregg	0+3	3
Emmanuel Eboue	159+55	214
Alexander Hleb	109+21	130
Alex Song	179+25	204
Fabrice Muamba	2	2
Anthony Stokes	0+1	1
Nicklas Bendtner	83+88	171
Kerrea Gilbert	10+2	12
Abou Diaby	136+44	180
Emmanuel Adebayor	114+28	142
Tomas Rosicky	158+88	246
Theo Walcott	252+145	397
William Gallas	142	142
Julio Baptista	17+18	35
Matthew Connolly	1+1	2
Denilson	120+33	153
Armand Traore	28+4	32
Mark Randall	4+9	13
Mart Poom	1+1	2

Career Record

Bacary Sagna	272+12	284
Eduardo	41+26	67
Lassana Diarra	8+5	13
Lukasz Fabianski	75+3	78
Fran Merida	7+9	16
Kieran Gibbs	183+47	230
Henri Lansbury	1+7	8
Nacer Barazite	0+3	3
Aaron Ramsey	237+92	329
Samir Nasri	110+15	125
Carlos Vela	19+43	62
Jack Wilshere	150+47	197
Gavin Hoyte	4	4
Francis Coquelin	115+45	160
Jay Simpson	1+2	3
Mikael Silvestre	37+6	43
Amaury Bischoff	0+4	4
Rui Fonte	0+1	1
Paul Rodgers	1	1
Andrey Arshavin	97+47	144
Vito Mannone	22+1	23
Thomas Vermaelen	136+14	150
Wojciech Szczesny	181	181
Sanchez Watt	1+2	3
Gilles Sunu	1+1	2
Craig Eastmond	7+3	10
Kyle Bartley	1	1
Thomas Cruise	1	1

Career Record

Jay Emmanuel-Thomas	1+4	5
Marouane Chamakh	36+31	67
Laurent Koscielny	318+6	324
Sebastien Squillaci	35+4	39
Ignasi Miquel	9+5	14
Conor Henderson	1	1
Gervinho	44+19	63
Emmanuel Frimpong	10+6	16
Carl Jenkinson	43+14	57
Alex Oxlade-Chamberlain	115+83	198
Per Mertesacker	215+6	221
Mikel Arteta	131+19	150
Yossi Benayoun	15+10	25
Andre Santos	21+12	33
Ju Young Park	4+3	7
Ryo Miyaichi	2+5	7
Oguzhan Ozyakup	0+2	2
Chuks Aneke	0+1	1
Nico Yennaris	2+2	4
Daniel Boateng	0+1	1
Santi Cazorla	166+14	180
Lukas Podolski	55+27	82
Olivier Giroud	169+84	253
Martin Angha	1+1	2
Emiliano Martinez	12+1	13
Serge Gnabry	9+9	18
Thomas Eisfeld	1+1	2
Jernade Meade	1+1	2

Nacho Monreal	187+25	212
Yaya Sanogo	9+11	20
Mesut Ozil	187+9	196
Chuba Akpom	1+11	12
Isaac Hayden	2	2
Kristoffer Olsson	0+1	1
Hector Bellerin	150+12	162
Gedion Zelalem	0+4	4
Kim Kallstrom	1+3	4
Mathieu Debuchy	29+1	30
Calum Chambers	57+26	83
Alexis Sanchez	153+13	166
Joel Campbell	23+17	40
Danny Welbeck	71+41	112
David Ospina	67+3	70
Ainsley Maitland-Niles	24+14	38
Stefan O'Connor	0+1	1
Gabriel Paulista	53+11	64
Petr Cech	117	117
Alex Iwobi	71+27	98
Glen Kamara	1	1
Ismael Bennacer	0+1	1
Krystian Bielik	0+2	2
Jeff Reine - Adelaide	5+3	8
Mohamed Elneny	52+20	72
Rob Holding	39+5	44
Granit Xhaka	85+9	94
Shkodran Mustafi	73+2	75

Lucas Perez	9+12	21
Chris Willock	0+2	2
Alexandre Lacazette	33+6	39
Sead Kolasinac	28+8	36
Reiss Nelson	8+8	16
Josh Dasilva	0+3	3
Joe Willock	6+5	11
Marcus McGuane	0+2	2
Eddie Nketiah	0+10	10
Ben Sheaf	0+2	2
Matt Macey	2	2
Henrikh Mkhitaryan	14+3	17
Pierre-E Aubameyang	13+1	14
Dinos Mavropanos	3	3

Wenger gave 83 graduates from the Arsenal Academy their first team debuts.

TOP TEN TRANSFER FEES PAID

1. Pierre-Emerick Aubameyang – £56m
2. Alexandre Lacazette – £47m
3. Mesut Ozil – £42.5m
4. Shkodran Mustafi – £35m
5. Granit Xhaka – £34m
6. Alexis Sanchez – £32m

7. Calum Chambers – £18m

8. Jose Antonio Reyes – £17.5m

9. Lucas Perez – £17.1m

10. Danny Welbeck – £16m

Total fees paid in transfers: £767m
Net spend: £349m

Source: Arsenal Database, Arsenal.com

INDEX

INDEX

INDEX

328

INDEX

INDEX

INDEX

INDEX

INDEX

PICTURE CREDITS

p.28 (above) © Getty/Laurence Griffiths; (below) Getty/ Paul Ellis

p.29 (below) © Getty/Adrian Dennis